# A TRANSLATOR'S GUIDE
# TO PAUL'S FIRST LETTER
# TO THE CORINTHIANS

# Helps For Translators Series

## Technical Helps:

Old Testament Quotations in the New Testament
Section Headings for the New Testament
Short Bible Reference System
New Testament Index
Orthography Studies
Bible Translations for Popular Use
The Theory and Practice of Translation
Bible Index
Fauna and Flora of the Bible
Short Index to the Bible
Manuscript Preparation
Marginal Notes for the Old Testament
Marginal Notes for the New Testament
The Practice of Translating

## Handbooks:

A Translator's Handbook on Ruth
A Translator's Handbook on the Book of Amos
A Translator's Handbook on the Book of Jonah
A Translator's Handbook on the Gospel of Mark
A Translator's Handbook on the Gospel of Luke
A Translator's Handbook on the Gospel of John
A Translator's Handbook on the Acts of the Apostles
A Translator's Handbook on Paul's Letter to the Romans
A Translator's Handbook on Paul's Letter to the Galatians
A Translator's Handbook on Paul's Letter to the Ephesians
A Translator's Handbook on Paul's Letter to the Philippians
A Translator's Handbook on Paul's Letters to the Colossians and to Philemon
A Translator's Handbook on Paul's Letters to the Thessalonians
A Translator's Handbook on the First Letter from Peter
A Translator's Handbook on the Letters of John

## Guides:

A Translator's Guide to Selections from the First Five Books of the Old Testament
A Translator's Guide to Selected Psalms
A Translator's Guide to the Gospel of Matthew
A Translator's Guide to the Gospel of Mark
A Translator's Guide to the Gospel of Luke
A Translator's Guide to Paul's First Letter to the Corinthians

HELPS FOR TRANSLATORS

# A TRANSLATOR'S GUIDE
## to
# PAUL'S FIRST LETTER
# TO THE CORINTHIANS

by
ROBERT G. BRATCHER

UNITED BIBLE SOCIETIES
London, New York,
Stuttgart

Books in the series of Helps for Translators may be ordered from a national Bible Society, or from either of the following centers:

United Bible Societies
European Production
Fund
D-7000 Stuttgart 80
Postfach 81 03 40
West Germany

American Bible Society
1865 Broadway
New York, New York 10023
U.S.A.

**L.C. Cataloging in Publication Data**

Bratcher, Robert G.
  A translator's guide to Paul's first letter to the Corinthians.

  (Helps for translators)
  Bibliography: p.
  Includes index.
  1. Bible. N.T. Corinthians, 1st--Translating.
I. Title. II. Series.
BS2675.2.B73          227'.2077          82-6951
ISBN 0-8267-0185-X                       AACR2

ABS-1982-1500-CM-08566

# Contents

# Preface

*A Translator's Guide to Paul's First Letter to the Corinthians* is
another volume in the series of Guides prepared as part of the general
series, *Helps for Translators*. The Handbooks were formerly the only
exegetical materials on various books of the Bible published by the
United Bible Societies for the use of translators.

The Handbooks have proven to be valuable for a good number of translators. They are full-range commentaries that deal with problems of the
original text, interpretation, vocabulary analysis, and discourse structure. They also include analyses of translation problems that may occur,
and they provide suggestions for dealing with such problems. Some translators, however, prefer material in a more condensed form and from which
they can easily retrieve information. Therefore the Translator's Guides
do not, for example, attempt to explain the reasons for the exegesis of
a passage nor for a suggested solution to a translation problem. A Guide
does not take away from translators the responsibility to make their own
decisions, but it does attempt to give them practical information and to
alert them to pitfalls they may otherwise overlook. It is hoped that such
information will enable a translator to prepare a translation that is
faithful to the meaning of the original and that is presented in a style
which is appropriate and effective in communicating the message to the
reader.

Other Guides are in preparation, covering material from both the Old
Testament and the New Testament. Meanwhile, preparation of the Handbooks
continues, so that the needs of all translators may be met. The United
Bible Societies Subcommittee on Translations will welcome any suggestions
for making both the Handbooks and the Guides more effective and useful
for translators.

# Abbreviations Used in This Volume

Books of the Bible:

| | | | |
|---|---|---|---|
| Col | Colossians | Lev | Leviticus |
| 1,2 Cor | 1,2 Corinthians | Matt | Matthew |
| Deut | Deuteronomy | Num | Numbers |
| Eph | Ephesians | Phil | Philippians |
| Exo | Exodus | Prov | Proverbs |
| Gal | Galatians | Rev | Revelation |
| Gen | Genesis | Rom | Romans |
| Heb | Hebrews | 1 Thes | 1 Thessalonians |
| Isa | Isaiah | | |

Other Abbreviations:

| | |
|---|---|
| B.C. | before Christ |
| KJV | King James Version |
| NEB | New English Bible |
| NIV | New International Version |
| RSV | Revised Standard Version |
| TEV | Today's English Version |

# Translating Paul's First Letter to the Corinthians

The purpose of this Guide is to help translators recognize and solve some of the problems they will encounter in translating this Letter. The Guide is not intended to replace standard commentaries or the forthcoming Handbook, which is also to be published by the United Bible Societies. Rather it seeks to show, in a simple and consistent way, what translators must do in order to provide in their own language a text that is faithful to the meaning of the original and that is clear and simple for the reader. Every translator is encouraged to seek additional help from available commentaries and Bible dictionaries, and to consult other translations.

The Letter is divided into sections, each with a heading that indicates the content or the main idea of the section. The translator should carefully read the whole section before starting to translate the first verse of the section.

The Guide uses the Today's English Version (TEV) section headings, and prints the text of both the TEV and the Revised Standard Version (RSV). The translator will notice that in many places the two are considerably different in form, although in the vast majority of instances the meaning is the same. The differences are due to the fact that the RSV is a translation that tries to reflect, as far as possible, the form of the original Greek, in terms of vocabulary, word classes, word order, and grammatical constructions. The TEV attempts to express the meaning of the Greek text as simply and naturally as possible, using a vocabulary and grammatical constructions that will be easily understood by most people who read English.

The translator is encouraged to imitate the TEV in this respect, and to express the meaning of the text in a form that will be easy for the reader to understand.

After each TEV section heading other suggestions are made for different ways to translate the heading.

After each verse, printed in full in both the TEV (left hand column) and the RSV (right hand column) texts, key passages are selected for explanation; these are underlined, and suggestions are given about other ways of translating. Where necessary, explanations are provided to enable the translator to understand better what is being proposed. Quotations from TEV are underlined, while quotations from RSV and other translations are in quotation marks.

The Guide takes notice of places where there are important differences among the Greek manuscripts of the Letter. In some places RSV and TEV differ in their decision on the Greek text (see 2.1); the Guide states the matter concisely and recommends what a translator should do.

Translating 1 Corinthians

The most important thing is that a translator be thoroughly ac-
quainted with a whole passage (a section or a chapter) before starting
to translate it, so as to reflect the author's style, the unity of the
passage, and the development of thought.

Outline of 1 Corinthians

A.  Introduction.  1.1-9

B.  Disorders in the Church.  1.10—6.20

    1. Dissensions.  1.10—4.21
    2. Immorality.  5.1-13
    3. Lawsuits among Believers.  6.1-8
    4. Christian Morality.  6.9-20

C.  Answers to Questions from Corinth.  7.1—16.4

    1.  Marriage and Celibacy.  7.1-40
    2.  Food Offered to Idols.  8.1—11.1
    3.  Church Life and Worship.  11.2—14.40
    4.  The Resurrection of Christ and of Believers.  15.1-58
    5.  The Offering for Fellow Believers in Judea.  16.1-4

D.  Personal Matters and Conclusion.  16.5-24

# Chapter 1

TEV has no section heading for the first three verses. One may be supplied, if needed: "Introduction," "Beginning of the Letter."

1.1                    TEV                                          RSV
    From Paul, who was called by          Paul, called by the will of
the will of God to be an apostle       God to be an apostle of Christ
of Christ Jesus, and from our          Jesus, and our brother Sosthenes,
brother Sosthenes—

    Verses 1-3 begin the letter with an identification of the writers (verse 1), of the readers (verse 2), and a prayer by the writers on behalf of the readers (verse 3).
    From Paul: "This letter is written by Paul," or "I, Paul, was called ...Christ Jesus. Our brother Sosthenes and I write this letter 2 to the church.... "
    called by the will of God: "it was God's own decision that I be an apostle, and so he called me to be an apostle." Or, more simply, "called by God"; or else, "designated" or "given the task."
    apostle: one who is given the commission to speak and act with the authority of the one who sent him. He is not merely a messenger; he has the authority to act on behalf of the one who sent him. The whole verbal phrase called...to be an apostle may be expressed by "God wanted (or, decided) it, and so he called me to speak and act...."
    an apostle of Christ Jesus: "an apostle to represent (or, speak for) Christ Jesus," or "an apostle who was sent out by Christ Jesus." It should be noticed that in Greek the order of the double name is Christ Jesus. In some languages this is either strange or unnatural, and so the order "Jesus Christ" is used.
    our brother: "our fellow Christian," "our fellow believer in Christ Jesus." The our is inclusive; it includes the whole Christian fellowship.
    Sosthenes: perhaps the one who appears in Acts 18.17. Paul seems to mention Sosthenes as an act of courtesy; Sosthenes does not appear to have a real part in the writing of the letter.

1.2                    TEV                                          RSV
    To the church of God which is          To the church of God which is
in Corinth, to all who are called      at Corinth, to those sanctified in
to be God's holy people, who belong    Christ Jesus, called to be saints
to him in union with Christ Jesus,     together with all those who in
together with all people everywhere    every place call on the name of

[ 3 ]

who worship our Lord Jesus Christ,     our Lord Jesus Christ, both their
their Lord and ours:                   Lord and ours:

the church of God: this is equivalent to saying "the people of
God." In the Old Testament the people of God are the people of Israel,
but in the New Testament they are the people who belong to God because
they have accepted Jesus as the Messiah and Lord. In the New Testament,
church always refers to people, never to a building. The phrase the
church of God may be represented by "the people in Corinth who belong
to God" or "...who worship God."

Corinth was one of the most important cities in Greece; at that
time it was in the Roman province of Achaia. For Paul's stay there see
Acts 18.1-18.

to all who are called: this additional explanation describes the
people of the church in Corinth, so it may be better to say "to all of
you who are called."

who are called to be God's holy people: TEV uses God's holy people
to represent the traditional "the saints" (see RSV). God is the one who
"calls," that is, who speaks to people through his messengers and in-
vites them to worship him, serve him, be his people. The adjective holy
has the Old Testament sense of dedicated to God, belonging to him, being
used for his purposes.

who belong to him in union with Christ Jesus: this translates the
expression "those sanctified in Christ Jesus" (RSV); the new element
here is "in Christ Jesus." Paul often uses this phrase (or "in Christ"
or "in the Lord") to express the closeness of the relationship between
believers and Christ. Not only do they belong to him or follow him, but
they are one with him. It is a vital, living relationship.

together with: this emphasizes the universal fellowship which includes Christians everywhere. But Paul is not writing this letter to
these other people—he is writing to the Christians in Corinth.

worship: this translates the expression "call on the name of" (RSV).
In the Bible "to call on the name" of God, or of Christ, is to pray to
him or worship him.

our Lord Jesus Christ: "Jesus Christ our Lord," "Jesus Christ, who
is our Lord." The our here includes all Christians.

their Lord and ours: here their refers to other Christians everywhere; ours refers to Paul (and Sosthenes) and the Christians in Corinth.

1.3             TEV                                RSV
     May God our Father and the Lord        Grace to you and peace from
Jesus Christ give you grace and        God our Father and the Lord Jesus
peace.                                 Christ.

May: in prayer this can be represented by, "I pray that," "I ask
that."

give you grace and peace: this is the standard form that Paul uses
in his letters. Grace is, first of all, God's great love and then the
good things, the blessings, he gives his people. Peace is not just the
absence of conflict or dispute, but the positive quality of well-being,
wholeness, salvation. The prayer may be represented by "I pray that God

[ 4 ]

will bless you and give you peace."

The whole introduction to the letter is one long sentence, and it may be restructured as follows:

> I, Paul, write this letter, together with our fellow believer (or, fellow Christian) Sosthenes. God himself chose me to be an apostle of Christ Jesus, that is, to go everywhere to proclaim his message. 2 I write this letter to the people in Corinth who belong to the church of God, that is, the people whom God has chosen to belong to him and to serve him. You are the people who belong to God because you are united with Christ Jesus. You are also united with all people everywhere who worship our Lord Jesus Christ, who is their Lord as well as our Lord. 3 I pray that God our Father and the Lord Jesus Christ will bless you and give you peace (or, well-being).

SECTION HEADING

Blessings in Christ: "The Good Things that God Gives Us through Jesus Christ."

In this section (1.4-9) Paul gives thanks to God for his fellow Christians in Corinth and mentions the many good things that God has given them.

| 1.4 TEV | RSV |
|---|---|
| I always give thanks to my God for you because of the grace he has given you through Christ Jesus. | I give thanks to God$^a$ always for you because of the grace of God which was given you in Christ Jesus, |
| | $^a$Other ancient authorities read *my God* |

I always give thanks: "I give thanks continually" or "...many times" or "...often." Or else, "Every time I pray I give thanks."

to my God: some Greek manuscripts have "to God" (see RSV). In some languages God cannot be possessed, so it is necessary to say "to the God I worship" or "...I serve."

because of the grace: this is the reason why Paul gives thanks to God. Here grace means "good things," "blessings," "(spiritual) gifts." In Paul's letters grace is (1) a disposition on God's part, his attitude of love, favor, kindness toward people (see 15.10); (2) the expression of that attitude: gifts, blessings (1.3); (3) the response on the believer's part: gratitude (see 10.30); and (4) the expression of that gratitude in the form of a gift (see 16.3).

through Christ Jesus: TEV has taken the Greek to mean that Christ Jesus is the one by whom God blessed the Christians in Corinth. But the Greek "in Christ Jesus" (RSV) could be taken to mean "in your union with Christ Jesus" (see 1.2) or "because you trust in Christ Jesus."

| 1.5 TEV | RSV |
|---|---|
| For in union with Christ you have become rich in all things, including all speech and all knowledge. | that in every way you were enriched in him with all speech and all knowledge— |

For in union with Christ: "Because you are united with Christ."

you have become rich in all things: this passive construction has God as the agent: "God has made you rich in all things." This is spiritual wealth, not material wealth: "spiritually wealthy in every way."

including all speech and all knowledge: instead of TEV including, the meaning could be "that is," which is to say that all speech and all knowledge are the all things which make the Corinthian Christians rich. This may be better than the TEV rendering. In this passage both speech and knowledge have a restricted sense. Paul is not talking about any and every kind of speech and knowledge, but about the proclamation of the Christian message and the understanding of the Christian message. Some translations reverse the two: "You have complete knowledge (of the Christian message) and you are able to proclaim it fully."

| 1.6 TEV | RSV |
|---|---|
| The message about Christ has become so firmly established in you | even as the testimony to Christ was confirmed among you— |

Notice that RSV places this verse between dashes, to show that the thought flows directly from verse 5 to verse 7.

The message about Christ: this translates the expression "The testimony (or, witness) of Christ." This could be taken to mean (1) the testimony that Christ gives, or (2) the testimony that others give about Christ. The latter is what is meant here: this is the Christian proclamation, the truth about Christ which is proclaimed by his followers.

firmly established in you: this refers to the way in which the believers in Corinth had received the message. "You have believed (or, accepted) completely the message about Christ," or "You have accepted... so strongly."

| 1.7 TEV | RSV |
|---|---|
| that you have not failed to receive a single blessing, as you wait for our Lord Jesus Christ to be revealed. | so that you are not lacking in any spiritual gift, as you wait for the revealing of our Lord Jesus Christ; |

that: in some languages the construction so...that may be difficult, and so it may be better to restructure as follows: "The message about Christ has become firmly established in you, and as a result...."

not failed to receive: this negative form may be represented in a positive fashion: "...that you have received every blessing," or "God has given you every blessing."

blessing: this translates a Greek word which is related to the word which means "grace." It means "a gift," "a good thing," which is the result of God's love for his people.

as you wait: this describes a vital aspect of the Christian life.
It looks forward to the future, when "our Lord Jesus Christ will be revealed." This "revelation" is the final and complete demonstration to
all humanity of his love and power, of his authority as Lord of all.

to be revealed: or "to reveal himself," "to demonstrate (to all)
who he is." Or, as in other passages, it is God who reveals: "for God
to reveal Jesus Christ," "...to show the authority (or, power) of Jesus
Christ."

| 1.8 | TEV | RSV |
|---|---|---|
| | He will also keep you firm to the end, so that you will be fault-less on the Day of our Lord Jesus Christ. | who will sustain you to the end, guiltless in the day of our Lord Jesus Christ. |

keep you firm to the end: "keep your faith from weakening," "keep
your faith strong."

the end: the day that Jesus Christ is revealed, the day when all
people will be judged by him.

you will be faultless: on that Day of Judgment no reason will be
found to condemn them; they will be acquitted, declared innocent;
they will not be condemned.

the Day of our Lord Jesus Christ: "the Day when our Lord Jesus
Christ comes (or, returns)." This will be the Day of Judgment, thought
of as taking place when the world comes to an end. Then God and Jesus
Christ will judge all humanity.

| 1.9 | TEV | RSV |
|---|---|---|
| | God is to be trusted, the God who called you to have fellowship with his Son Jesus Christ, our Lord. | God is faithful, by whom you were called into the fellowship of his Son, Jesus Christ our Lord. |

God is to be trusted: or "God is faithful" (RSV). "We can trust
God to keep his promises," "We are certain that God will do what he
said he would."

the God who called you: this translates a passive expression in
Greek (see RSV).

to have fellowship with his Son: this is another way of expressing
the relationship expressed by the phrase "union with Christ" (see
verse 2).

our Lord: the our includes all Christians.

SECTION HEADING

Divisions in the Church: "Paul Condemns the Disputes in the Church."
In this section (1.10-17) Paul condemns the different factions which
have appeared in the church in Corinth, shows how senseless and wrong
they are, and asks the Corinthian Christians to unite in their common

1.10

loyalty to Christ.


<table>
<tr><td>1.10</td><td>TEV</td><td>RSV</td></tr>
</table>

| | |
|---|---|
| By the authority of our Lord Jesus Christ I appeal to all of you, my brothers, to agree in what you say, so that there will be no divisions among you. Be completely united, with only one thought and one purpose. | I appeal to you, brethren, by the name of our Lord Jesus Christ, that all of you agree and that there be no dissensions among you, but that you be united in the same mind and the same judgment. |

By the authority of our Lord Jesus Christ: "Because of the authority that the Lord Jesus Christ has given me," "The Lord Jesus Christ has given me authority, and so I appeal to you." Here authority translates the Greek "name" (see RSV).

my brothers: "my fellow believers," "my fellow Christians," "my brothers and sisters." Paul is not excluding women; the term brothers includes all the people in the church at Corinth.

agree in what you say: or "agree among yourselves," "be in agreement with one another." The appeal may be phrased as follows: "I appeal ...to be completely united in your speech, thought, and purpose, so that the divisions among you will disappear."

Be completely united: "Be in complete accord."

with only one thought and one purpose: "agree about what you think and what you want."


<table>
<tr><td>1.11</td><td>TEV</td><td>RSV</td></tr>
</table>

| | |
|---|---|
| For some people from Chloe's family have told me quite plainly, my brothers, that there are quarrels among you. | For it has been reported to me by Chloe's people that there is quarreling among you, my brethren. |

Chloe is a woman, a member of the church in Corinth. Chloe's family translates "some (or, those) of Chloe," which may be understood as "Chloe's household," that is, including servants or slaves, and not just members of her family.

have told me quite plainly: this assumes that the passive "it was made known to me" (see RSV) means that those people had gone to Paul and spoken with him; but the information might have been communicated by means of a letter.

quarrels: "factions," "rivalries," "divisions," "dissensions."


<table>
<tr><td>1.12</td><td>TEV</td><td>RSV</td></tr>
</table>

| | |
|---|---|
| Let me put it this way: each one of you says something different. One says, "I follow Paul"; another, "I follow Apollos"; another, "I follow Peter"; and another, "I follow Christ." | What I mean is that each one of you says, "I belong to Paul," or "I belong to Apollos," or "I belong to Cephas," or "I belong to Christ." |

Let me put it this way: "This is what I mean," or "...I am talking about."

each one of you says something different: or "different things are said by different people," or "there are groups (or, factions) which say different things." Paul mentions four different groups.

I follow Paul: "I belong to the group that honors Paul," "I accept the authority of Paul."

Apollos: a Christian leader who had preached the gospel in Corinth (see Acts 18.24—19.1).

Peter: one of the twelve apostles. The Greek text has the Aramaic form of his name, "Cephas" (see RSV).

| 1.13 TEV | RSV |
|---|---|
| Christ has been divided$^a$ into groups! Was it Paul who died on the cross for you? Were you baptized as Paul's disciples? | Is Christ divided? Was Paul crucified for you? Or were you baptized in the name of Paul? |

$^a$Christ has been divided; *some manuscripts have* Christ cannot be divided.

Christ has been divided into groups: the Greek text may be punctuated as a rhetorical question (RSV) or as a statement (TEV). Paul is saying that the loyalty of believers to Christ cannot be divided among others, but must go exclusively to Christ; so when different factions appear in a church, the result is a division of Christ himself, who is identified with his followers. The unity of Christ has been broken up into pieces. In some languages the figure of Christ being broken into different parts may be impossible to express, and so the meaning may be represented by "Christ is no longer the one and only leader all of you are following," "You are acting as though there were many Christs, not just one."

Textual Note: some Greek manuscripts have the negative adverb "not," with the resulting meaning "Christ has not been divided" or "Christ cannot be divided" (TEV footnote).

Was it Paul...?: this is a rhetorical question, stating what is obviously not so: "Paul was not crucified for you," or "I, Paul, was not crucified for you."

Were you baptized as Paul's disciples?: another rhetorical question, again a denial: "You were not baptized as Paul's disciples." The Greek phrase "in the name of Paul" (RSV) may be taken to mean "by Paul's authority."

baptized: this Christian rite was accomplished by immersing converts in water. Usually there is one term for this rite used by the various Christian communions, and a translation should use this word or expression.

| 1.14 TEV | RSV |
|---|---|
| I thank God that I did not bap-tize any of you except Crispus and Gaius. | I am thankful*b* that I baptized none of you except Crispus and Gaius; |

*b*Other ancient authorities read
*I thank God*

I thank God: as the RSV text and footnote show, the Greek text may have been "I am thankful." It is impossible to be sure which one is original.
Crispus: see Acts 18.8.
Gaius: perhaps the man named in Romans 16.23 as Paul's host while he was in Corinth.

| 1.15 TEV | RSV |
|---|---|
| No one can say, then, that you were baptized as my disciples. | lest any one should say that you were baptized in my name. |

you were baptized as my disciples: or "you were baptized by my authority" (as in verse 13).

| 1.16 TEV | RSV |
|---|---|
| (Oh yes, I also baptized Stephanas and his family; but I can't re-member whether I baptized anyone else.) | (I did baptize also the household of Stephanas. Beyond that, I do not know whether I baptized any one else.) |

TEV places this verse between parentheses since Paul is here cor-recting the statement that he had baptized only Crispus and Gaius.
Stephanas and his family: or "Stephanas and the members of his household" (including servants and slaves). See also 16.15-16.

| 1.17 TEV | RSV |
|---|---|
| Christ did not send me to baptize. He sent me to tell the Good News, and to tell it without using the language of human wisdom, in order to make sure that Christ's death on the cross is not robbed of its power. | For Christ did not send me to baptize but to preach the gospel, and not with eloquent wisdom, lest the cross of Christ be emptied of its power. |

Christ did not send me to baptize: the verb send here is related to the noun "apostle," which means "one who is sent." "Christ did not make me his apostle in order for me to baptize people." Paul is not say-ing that he could not baptize; he is saying that his primary function as an apostle is not to baptize.

to tell the Good News: "to proclaim the gospel," "to spread the Christian message." If a word for "preach" is used (see RSV), it should not imply a formal discourse delivered in a worship service in church.

without using the language of human wisdom: Paul has much to say about human wisdom in this letter. What he means is that when he proclaims the Christian message, he does not use the language of Greek philosophy, with its mode of reasoning, inferences, deductions, and conclusions. The statement may be rephrased: "to tell it without using words based on human wisdom." The truth of the Gospel is not established by human reason and logic, but by God's wisdom, revealed in Christ crucified (see verses 21-25).

in order to make sure that: "so that," "for the purpose of."

Christ's death on the cross: this translates the Greek "the cross of Christ" (see RSV). TEV has felt it necessary to say Christ's death on the cross since Paul is obviously not speaking of the wooden construction itself but of Christ's crucifixion.

robbed of its power: "become something useless," "become an empty (or, weak) matter."

The English negative passive expression is not robbed may be difficult to translate literally. It may be better to restructure the whole sentence as follows: "He sent me to tell (or, proclaim) the Good News. As I proclaim the Good News (or, As I do so), I do not use the language of human logic. If I did, my message would take away the real power of Christ's death on the cross." Or, "If I did, then (the message about) Christ's death on the cross would not be powerful."


SECTION HEADING

Christ the Power and the Wisdom of God: "In Christ We See the Power and the Wisdom of God," "The Power and Wisdom of God Are Shown in Christ." In this section (1.18-31) Paul develops the theme of God's power and God's wisdom. Both were clearly shown in Christ's death on the cross.

It would be possible, and perhaps better, to limit this section to verses 18-25 and to make verses 26-31 another section—for which an appropriate heading will be suggested at verse 26.


| 1.18     TEV | RSV |
|---|---|
| For the message about Christ's death on the cross is nonsense to those who are being lost; but for us who are being saved it is God's power. | For the word of the cross is folly to those who are perishing, but to us who are being saved it is the power of God. |

Paul now justifies what he said in verse 17. He explains why the language of human reason and logic does not serve to proclaim the Christian message.

the message about Christ's death on the cross: this translates the Greek "the word (or, message) of the cross" (see RSV). The fuller form brings out more clearly the meaning of Paul's words.

is nonsense: "means nothing," "has no meaning," "is foolish."

those who are being lost: "those who are on their way to perdition
(or, condemnation)." The Greek participle "dying" (RSV "perishing")
refers to people who are dying spiritually, on their way to spiritual
death. It does not mean merely "losing their way."

for us who are being saved: us is inclusive, "all of us." The passive participle being saved has God for agent: "for us whom God is saving," "for us who are being saved by God." The present tense describes
salvation as a process, as an ongoing activity.

is God's power: the construction the message...is God's power may
be impossible in some languages. Paul does not merely mean that the
Christian message is about God's power; he means that for Christians
the message is a manisfestation of God's power, a means whereby God's
power becomes effective in human lives and history. Perhaps something
like "the message...demonstrates (or, is an instrument of) the power of
God," or "for us whom God is saving the message shows his power."

| 1.19 TEV | RSV |
|---|---|
| The scripture says,<br>"I will destroy the wisdom of<br>    the wise<br>  and set aside the<br>    understanding of the<br>    scholars." | For it is written,<br>"I will destroy the wisdom of<br>    the wise,<br>  and the cleverness of the clever<br>    I will thwart." |

To prove his point, Paul cites Isaiah 29.14, following the ancient
Greek version, the Septuagint; the Hebrew text has "the wisdom of their
wise men will perish, and the understanding of their prudent men will be
hid."

I will destroy: here God is the speaker, so it may be well to say
"God will destroy." Or else, "In the scripture God says, 'I will destroy...'" or "In the scripture we read that God said....'"

destroy the wisdom of the wise: "bring the wisdom of wise people
to nothing," "show (or, prove) that the wisdom of wise people means
nothing (or, is useless)."

set aside the understanding of the scholars: this line repeats, in
different fashion, the same thought of the previous line. It may be
preferable to express the meaning in one statement: "God will show (or,
prove) that all human wisdom and understanding mean nothing (or, are of
no value)."

| 1.20 TEV | RSV |
|---|---|
| So then, where does that leave the<br>wise? or the scholars? or the skill-<br>ful debaters of this world? God has<br>shown that this world's wisdom is<br>foolishness! | Where is the wise man? Where is<br>the scribe? Where is the debater<br>of this age? Has not God made<br>foolish the wisdom of the world? |

So then, where does that leave...?: this is a rhetorical question,
meaning that the wise, the scholars, the skillful debaters have nothing
to say about God's power and wisdom. It may be necessary to recast the

questions as a statement: "This means that the wise people, and the scholars, and the skillful debaters have nothing worthwhile (or, sensible) to say (about God's power)." If rhetorical questions are used in the receptor language, the translator should use one here, as long as the rhetorical nature of the question is clear.

skillful debaters of this world: "people who are clever with arguments." The qualification of this world (RSV "of this age") is added in order to emphasize the orientation of the people Paul is criticizing; their thinking is dominated by purely human, or worldly, values. The Greek word for "age" reflects the Jewish concept of two ages, or periods, in the history of mankind: the time before and the time after the coming of Messiah. But for the New Testament writers, the old "age" did not end with the beginning of the new age in Jesus Christ. The old age still exists, and it is inhabited by those who do not live according to the new age inaugurated by Jesus Christ. So "this age" has the meaning of purely human values, human philosophy, a worldly point of view. Those who have accepted Jesus Christ as Savior and Lord already live in the new age, the age of God's wisdom and power.

God has shown that this world's wisdom is foolishness: this translates a rhetorical question in Greek (see RSV). "God has reduced to foolishness the wisdom of people of this world." Here the Greek "this world" means the same as "this age" in the previous sentence.

| 1.21 TEV | RSV |
|---|---|
| For God in his wisdom made it impossible for people to know him by means of their own wisdom. Instead, by means of the so-called "foolish" message we preach, God decided to save those who believe. | For since, in the wisdom of God, the world did not know God through wisdom, it pleased God through the folly of what we preach to save those who believe. |

Here Paul contrasts God's wisdom with human wisdom.

God in his wisdom made it impossible: "God is truly wise and he made it impossible."

to know him: "to know him as he really is," "to know what he is truly like." As the next sentence makes clear, "to know God" means "to believe what he says and be saved." Knowledge of God is more than intellectual understanding; it is to be related to him through faith.

Translators may need to restructure the first part of this verse as follows: "God is wise and he made it so that people would not be able to know him."

the so-called "foolish" message we preach: the Christian message is thought to be foolishness by those who follow the world's way of reasoning; this is why TEV has so-called "foolish." This may be said, "the message we preach, which others (or, people of this world) call foolish." From the human point of view, what Christians say about Christ's crucifixion is nonsense.

those who believe: if an object must be supplied, it may be "believe God," or "believe in Christ," or "believe the Christian message."

1.22

| 1.22 TEV | RSV |
|---|---|
| Jews want miracles for proof, and Greeks look for wisdom. | For Jews demand signs and Greeks seek wisdom. |

Paul divides the human race into Jews and Greeks, and shows how the Christian message makes no sense to them.

want miracles for proof: the Greek is "ask for signs" (see RSV). These "signs" are unusual, supernatural events, miracles, which prove that the message is really from God.

Greeks: in contrast with Jews they are all other races, Gentiles (as the next verse makes clear). But the use of the word Greeks is especially relevant in this letter to Greek people. A translation might prefer to say "Gentiles" or "non-Jews" as being clearer than Greeks.

look for wisdom: "make wisdom their goal," "see wisdom as the most important thing."

| 1.23 TEV | RSV |
|---|---|
| As for us, we proclaim the crucified Christ, a message that is offensive to the Jews and nonsense to the Gentiles; | but we preach Christ crucified, a stumbling block to Jews and folly to Gentiles, |

As for us, we: this is emphatic in Greek. The we may refer to Paul's own preaching (and that of his companions) or else it may refer to all Christians. The former seems preferable.

we proclaim the crucified Christ: "our message is about Christ who was crucified."

offensive: this translates a Greek word which means "stumbling block" (RSV). It is something that prevents a person from following the path, that gets in a person's way, that leads a person astray or trips him up as he walks along. Here it means that what Christians say about the crucifixion of Jesus is so strange that Jews are shocked or offended by it.

nonsense: as in verse 18.
Gentiles: the same as Greeks in verse 22.

| 1.24 TEV | RSV |
|---|---|
| but for those whom God has called, both Jews and Gentiles, this message is Christ, who is the power of God and the wisdom of God. | but to those who are called, both Jews and Greeks, Christ the power of God and the wisdom of God. |

whom God has called: God "calls" people to believe in him, obey him, worship him, become his people.

this message is Christ: or "this message is about Christ," or "Christ is the message we proclaim."

who is the power of God and the wisdom of God: "who demonstrates what God's power is and what God's wisdom is," or "who shows how powerful and wise God really is." Christ is God's wise way of saving people, his power to save people.

1.25      TEV

For what seems to be God's foolishness is wiser than human wisdom,
and what seems to be God's weakness is stronger than human strength.

RSV

For the foolishness of God is
wiser than men, and the weakness
of God is stronger than men.

what seems to be God's foolishness: this translates "the foolishness of God" (RSV). TEV has what seems to be to make clear that it is
really not foolishness, but only from a human point of view, that is,
the point of view of Greeks (Gentiles), who admire human wisdom.
     what seems to be God's weakness: from the point of view of the
Jews, who require great miracles as signs of God's power.


1.26      TEV

     Now remember what you were, my
brothers, when God called you. From
the human point of view few of you
were wise or powerful or of high
social standing.

RSV

     For consider your call,
brethren; not many of you were
wise according to worldly standards, not many were powerful,
not many were of noble birth;

     In verses 26-31 Paul directly addresses the Corinthian Christians,
reminding them of their low social standing, emphasizing still the
qualities of foolishness and weakness, which clearly prove the wisdom
and the power of God to save people. If a translator decides to have
another section here, a heading may be "How God Saves People," or "God's
Power and Human Weakness."
     remember what you were...when God called you: "remember your condi-
tion (or, situation)...when God saved you." For called see verse 24.
     From the human point of view: this translates the Greek phrase
"according to the flesh"; the meaning is "by human standards," "according to worldly standards," "the way people judge things."
     of high social standing: "of noble birth," "aristocrats."


1.27      TEV

God purposely chose what the world
considers nonsense in order to
shame the wise, and he chose what
the world considers weak in order
to shame the powerful.

RSV

but God chose what is foolish in
the world to shame the wise, God
chose what is weak in the world
to shame the strong,

     what: this translates the Greek neuter pronoun. In this context,
however, it refers to persons, and so a better translation would be
"the people the world considers fools," or else "those that most people
consider to be fools."
     to shame the wise: "to discredit those who are wise," "to show
that wise people are not really wise."
     what the world considers weak: "those that the people of the world
look on as weak (or, powerless)."
     to shame the powerful: "to discredit those who are powerful," "to

prove that powerful people are not really powerful" or "...that their power is only an illusion."


| 1.28 TEV | RSV |
|---|---|
| He chose what the world looks down on and despises and thinks is nothing, in order to destroy what the world thinks is important. | God chose what is low and despised in the world, even things that are not, to bring to nothing things that are, |

what the world looks down on: this translates the Greek "those of humble birth," "lowly born" (as contrasted with "those of noble birth" in verse 26).

and thinks is nothing: RSV has the literal "even things that are not." Again, this applies to people, so one may translate "people whom the world looks down on and thinks are nothing."

Textual Note: TEV translates a Greek text that has the conjunction "and"; but many Greek manuscripts do not have "and," so that the expression ("things that are not") is a summary of all that precedes, not an additional classification. This text may be what Paul wrote.

thinks is important: this translates "things that are," the exact opposite of "things that are not." Again, Paul means "people whom the world considers important."

The whole verse may be translated: "God chose people of low social standing, by the world's standards, and people who are despised; in sum, the people whom the world regards as nothing are the very ones God chose. He did this in order to discredit those who are important, from a human point of view." Or, "...in order to show that those who from a human point of view are important are really not important."


| 1.29 TEV | RSV |
|---|---|
| This means that no one can boast in God's presence. | so that no human being might boast in the presence of God. |

This means: "The result is," "Because of this."

boast in God's presence: "boast in God's sight." Or, otherwise stated, "From God's point of view, no human being has a right to boast." But the Greek "before God" may refer to the Day of Judgment.


| 1.30 TEV | RSV |
|---|---|
| But God has brought you into union with Christ Jesus, and God has made Christ to be our wisdom. By him we are put right with God; we become God's holy people and are set free. | He is the source of your life in Christ Jesus, whom God made our wisdom, our righteousness and sanctification and redemption; |

God has brought you: "God is the one who has made you belong to Christ Jesus."

union with Christ Jesus: see 1.2.

The rest of the verse says, quite literally, in Greek: "God has made him (that is, Christ Jesus) our wisdom, and righteousness and sanctification and redemption" (see RSV). To take each word in order:

"our wisdom": to say "Christ Jesus is our wisdom" may not mean much. Instead, "He is the one who makes us truly wise" or "He is the one who shows us how God is wise."

"righteousness": "He is the one who puts us into the right relationship with God."

"sanctification": "He makes us God's people," "We are God's people because of what he has done for us." See holy people in 1.2.

"redemption": "He saves us," "He sets us free (from our sins)."

All of this may be phrased as follows: "It is through Christ that God makes us wise, puts us right into himself, makes us his own people, and sets us free from our sins."

| 1.31 | TEV | RSV |
|---|---|---|

So then, as the scripture says, "Whoever wants to boast must boast of what the Lord has done."

therefore, as it is written, "Let him who boasts, boast of the Lord."

the scripture: Paul cites Jeremiah 9.24 in summary form.

must boast of what the Lord has done: or "must boast of his relationship with the Lord." Here Lord refers to Christ Jesus. Since this is a quotation from the Old Testament the translator should not say "Jesus" in the text.

# Chapter 2

The Message about the Crucified Christ: "Paul's Message about Christ."

In this section (2.1-5) Paul writes about his ministry in Corinth. The theme of his message in Corinth was Christ crucified, and Paul's delivery of the message was in keeping with the theme. God's power did not manifest itself in the apostle's skill and wisdom but in his weakness.

| 2.1 TEV | RSV |
|---|---|
| When I came to you, my brothers, to preach God's secret truth,$^b$ I did not use big words and great learning. | When I came to you, brethren, I did not come proclaiming to you the testimony$^c$ of God in lofty words or wisdom. |
| $^b$God's secret truth; *some manuscripts have* the testimony about God. | $^c$Other ancient authorities read *mystery* (or *secret*) |

came: or "went."

my brothers: see 1.10.

God's secret truth: "the message from God that had not been known until now," "the truth about God which only now do we know." The real truth about God had been hidden but is now known in the Christian message; the real message from God is the one that is proclaimed through Jesus Christ. See further in verse 7.

Textual Note: as the TEV footnote and the RSV text show, some Greek manuscripts have "the testimony of God." The meaning of this phrase is "the testimony (or, witness) about God."

I did not use big words and great learning: or "I did not put on a great (or, impressive) display of eloquence and wisdom."

| 2.2 TEV | RSV |
|---|---|
| For while I was with you, I made up my mind to forget everything except Jesus Christ and especially his death on the cross. | For I decided to know nothing among you except Jesus Christ and him crucified. |

to forget everything except: in his preaching Paul concentrated on one thing only: Jesus Christ and especially his death on the cross. The main emphasis of Paul's preaching about Jesus was his crucifixion: "I made up my mind to pay attention to (or emphasize) Jesus Christ, and especially...."

2.3          TEV                                    RSV
So when I came to you, I was weak    And I was with you in weakness
and trembled all over with fear,     and in much fear and trembling;

Paul describes the feelings he had when he had proclaimed the gospel in Corinth: "weakness, fear, and much trembling." Paul uses vivid language in order to impress his readers that he did not rely on his own intellect or speaking ability, his own skill and power. The language of the apostle should be retained in translation: "I was weak and afraid, and I was shaking with fear."

2.4          TEV                                    RSV
and my teaching and message were     and my speech and my message were
not delivered with skillful words    not in plausible words of wisdom,
of human wisdom, but with con-       but in demonstration of the Spirit
vincing proof of the power of God's  and of power,
Spirit.

my teaching and message: the two words are related in meaning. Either (1) the first one has to do with the (oral) form of Paul's preaching and the second one with the content of his message, or (2) the two words mean the same, that is, the message as such.
skillful words of human wisdom: the adjective skillful translates a Greek word whose exact form and meaning are uncertain: "persuasive, convincing, reasonable"; RSV "plausible." The whole statement may be translated "When I taught and preached, I did not try to convince you (or, win you over) with arguments based on human wisdom...."
convincing proof of the power of God's Spirit: this translates the Greek "a demonstration of spirit and power." TEV takes "spirit and power" to mean "the power of the Spirit." This part of the verse may be recast as a sentence: "Instead, I delivered my message in a way that proved how powerful the Spirit of God is."

2.5          TEV                                    RSV
Your faith, then, does not rest      that your faith might not rest
on human wisdom but on God's         in the wisdom of men but in the
power.                               power of God.

Your faith: either "Your faith in God" or "Your faith in Christ."
does not rest on: "is not based on," "is not the result of," "is not caused by." "It was not because of human wisdom that you have come to trust in Christ, but because of God's power."

SECTION HEADING

God's Wisdom: "God's Wisdom Is Given Us by the Holy Spirit."
In this section (2.6-16) Paul defines the nature of God's wisdom and how it is made known to believers. God's wisdom is different from human wisdom, and only God's Spirit is able to understand it. So human

[ 19 ]

beings can know God's wisdom only by the action of the Spirit of God.

| 2.6    TEV | RSV |
|---|---|
| Yet I do proclaim a message of wisdom to those who are spiritually mature. But it is not the wisdom that belongs to this world or to the powers that rule this world—powers that are losing their power. | Yet among the mature we do impart wisdom, although it is not a wisdom of this age or of the rulers of this age, who are doomed to pass away. |

I do proclaim: this translates the Greek plural "we proclaim" (see RSV). Throughout this section the verbs and the first person pronouns are plural, not singular. It is to be noticed that TEV uses the singular in verses 6-7, but from verse 10 on TEV has plural. RSV always follows the Greek plural forms. TEV takes the plurals in verses 6-7 as epistolary plurals, that is, a literary device by means of which the writer refers to himself alone. If, however, a translation prefers to use a plural form in verses 6-7, it would be an exclusive plural, referring to Paul and his colleagues, not to Paul and the readers of the letter.

a message of wisdom: or "wisdom." The verb proclaim makes it reasonable to assume that message is what is meant as the object of the verb. The phrase message of wisdom may be taken to mean "a wise message" (a message that contains wisdom) or "a message about wisdom." The former seems more likely.

spiritually mature: this translates the Greek adjective for "perfect, complete, mature." Paul is not talking about physical maturity in terms of age, but of spiritual maturity, that is, the capacity to understand spiritual truths.

the wisdom that belongs to: "the wisdom that is taught by," or "the wisdom that this world and the powers that rule this world possess."

this world: or "this age"; see 1.20.

the powers that rule this world: Paul is not speaking specifically of human authorities (not even in verse 8, below), but rather of evil spiritual powers, thought of as angels or spirits (see Col 1.16; Eph 6. 12). They exercise their power through human beings, but human rulers and authorities are not themselves, as such, the powers that rule this world.

powers that are losing their power: "powers that are disappearing," "powers that are being defeated." Although these spiritual rulers have power, yet with the coming of Christ they are being defeated and will eventually vanish.

| 2.7    TEV | RSV |
|---|---|
| The wisdom I proclaim is God's secret wisdom, which is hidden from mankind, but which he had already chosen for our glory even before the world was made. | But we impart a secret and hidden wisdom of God, which God decreed before the ages for our glorification. |

God's secret wisdom, which is hidden from mankind: or else "God's secret wisdom, which has been hidden from mankind." Only in the Christian message is God's wisdom made known. It is known by those who accept the message, but it is unknown by others.

he had already chosen...even before the world was made: "he had already decided to reveal...before time began" or "...before he created the world." The Greek phrase "before the ages" (RSV) means before the creation of the world. All of past history is summarized by "the ages."

for our glory: here the Greek word for "glory" refers to God's saving work on behalf of mankind, his activity to restore mankind to the state of being the true children of God, sharing his nature ("glory") as it is revealed in Jesus. Human sin has destroyed that relationship (Rom 3.23), but it is restored by Christ (Col 1.27). Our is inclusive. The second part of the verse may be rephrased, "...but which he had already chosen for us before the world was made, so that we may be able to share in the very life of God."

| 2.8 TEV | RSV |
|---|---|
| None of the rulers of this world knew this wisdom. If they had known it, they would not have crucified the Lord of glory. | None of the rulers of this age understood this; for if they had, they would not have crucified the Lord of glory. |

rulers of this world: the spiritual rulers (as in verse 6).

they would not have crucified: of course Christ was crucified by human beings, soldiers under the power of the Roman authorities. But these human authorities were controlled by the spiritual powers, evil powers which did not recognize the meaning of Christ's death on the cross.

the Lord of glory: this title is applied to Jesus as the one who has God's "glory," that is, God's saving power, and also as the one who reveals God's saving power to mankind. It may be impossible to use such a phrase in translation, so it may be necessary to say "the Lord who has God's glory" or "the Lord who manifests God's glory." The sentence may be restructured: "They (The spiritual powers) crucified the Lord, the one who manifests God's saving power, because they did not know God's wisdom."

| 2.9 TEV | RSV |
|---|---|
| However, as the scripture says,<br>"What no one ever saw or<br>heard,<br>what no one ever thought<br>could happen,<br>is the very thing God<br>prepared for ·those who<br>love him." | But, as it is written,<br>"What no eye has seen, nor<br>ear heard, nor the heart of<br>man conceived, what God has<br>prepared for those who love<br>him," |

Paul quotes as scripture a passage that is related to Isaiah 64.4 (see also Isa 52.15). As it appears here, it emphasizes the fact that

God, through Jesus Christ, has done something completely different, something no human being could ever imagine would happen. The quotation may be restructured: "That which God has prepared (or, done) for those who love him is something no one ever saw or heard, something no one ever thought would (or, could) happen."

| 2.10    TEV | RSV |
|---|---|
| But$^c$ it was to us that God made known his secret by means of his Spirit. The Spirit searches everything, even the hidden depths of God's purposes. | God has revealed to us through the Spirit. For the Spirit searches everything, even the depths of God. |

$^c$But; *some manuscripts have* For.

The Greek text translated by TEV has But at the beginning of the verse; some manuscripts have For. Either one makes sense, but the meaning of Paul's comment seems to make But more fitting. It is to be noticed that RSV punctuates differently, making verses 9-10a one sentence. RSV's translation, no less than TEV, is a valid translation of the Greek text, so either translation may be followed.

to us: here it would seem that us is all-inclusive, that is, it refers to all Christians, those who have learned God's plan in Christ Jesus.

by means of his Spirit: or "through the (Holy) Spirit."

searches: "explores," "probes," "investigates"; or else, "knows."

the hidden depths of God's purposes: this translates the Greek "the depths of God" (RSV). Or else, "the hidden depths of God's thoughts (or, desires)," or "the deepest secret thoughts (or, plans) of God."

| 2.11    TEV | RSV |
|---|---|
| It is only a person's own spirit within him that knows all about him; in the same way, only God's Spirit knows all about God. | For what person knows a man's thoughts except the spirit of the man which is in him? So also no one comprehends the thoughts of God except the Spirit of God. |

Paul here draws an analogy between the human spirit, which alone knows the full truth about what a person thinks and wants, and God's Spirit.

a person's own spirit within him: here it may be difficult to have a word for the human spirit, that is, the center of self-awareness, that does not mean ghost or else simply desire or volition. A descriptive phrase may be needed, but it should match precisely the relation between God and his (Holy) Spirit. The verse may be restructured: "Who knows everything about a person? Only that person's own spirit (or, inner being). In the same way, only God's Spirit (or, the Spirit in God) knows everything about God."

2.12     TEV
We have not received this world's
spirit; instead, we have received
the Spirit sent by God, so that we
may know all that God has given us.

RSV
Now we have received not the spirit
of the world, but the Spirit which
is from God, that we might understand the gifts bestowed on us by
God.

Here Paul uses the same word spirit in a different sense: "the
spirit of the world." Here the word means the ability to perceive spiritual truth, which Paul describes as the spirit that governs people who
belong to this "age." The opening part of the verse may be translated,
"We (Christians) do not have within us the spirit that governs (the
people who belong to) this world."

so that we may know: "in order that we may understand." The purpose expressed by so that is related to God's action in sending his
Spirit. "God sent us his Spirit so that we may know...."

This comment about understanding leads directly to the thought
developed in verse 13.

all that God has given us: "the gifts that we have received from
God."

2.13     TEV
So then, we do not speak in
words taught by human wisdom, but
in words taught by the Spirit, as
we explain spiritual truths to
those who have the Spirit.$^d$

$^d$to those who have the Spirit;
 *or* with words given by the
 Spirit.

RSV
And we impart this in words not
taught by human wisdom but taught
by the Spirit, interpreting spiritual truths to those who possess
the Spirit.$^d$

$^d$Or *interpreting spiritual truths
 in spiritual language;* or *comparing spiritual things with
 spiritual*

It follows that those who proclaim God's message are ruled by
the Spirit of God: they know what God has done and so their message is
determined by the Spirit of God.

we: the Christian messengers, that is, Paul and his colleagues. Or
here this plural could represent Paul: "I."

words taught by human wisdom: "words inspired by human wisdom,"
"words that are the product of human wisdom."

as we explain spiritual truths to those who have the Spirit: as the
TEV and the RSV texts and footnotes show, the final words of the Greek
text may be understood in various ways. The Greek participle translated
as we explain (RSV "interpreting") may be taken to mean "comparing" (as
it does in 2 Cor 10.12); but in this context such meaning seems most unlikely. In some languages it will be better to reverse the order found
in TEV: "When we explain...the Spirit, we do not speak...."

The interpretation found in the TEV footnote is just as defensible
as the one in the TEV text; most translations prefer the meaning expressed in the TEV text.

| 2.14 TEV | RSV |
|---|---|
| Whoever does not have the Spirit cannot receive the gifts that come from God's Spirit. Such a person really does not understand them; they are nonsense to him, because their value can be judged only on a spiritual basis. | The unspiritual[e] man does not receive the gifts of the Spirit of God, for they are folly to him, and he is not able to understand them because they are spiritually discerned. |

*e*Or *natural*

**Whoever does not have the Spirit**: this translates the Greek "a natural person," that is, a human being governed by his own natural, human powers, and not by the Spirit of God. It stands in obvious contrast with those who have the Spirit in the preceding verse and so is translated "unspiritual man" by RSV.

**cannot receive**: or "rejects," "refuses to accept"; or "cannot apprehend," "cannot make use of."

**their value can be judged**: or "their meaning (or, purpose) can be understood."

**on a spiritual basis**: "from a spiritual point of view." Here as elsewhere, spiritual refers to the Spirit of God.

| 2.15 TEV | RSV |
|---|---|
| Whoever has the Spirit, however, is able to judge the value of everything, but no one is able to judge him. | The spiritual man judges all things, but is himself to be judged by no one. |

**to judge the value**: or "to understand the purpose (or, meaning)." This is the same verb that appears in the preceding verse.

**to judge him**: "to pass judgment on him." The meaning here is that no unspiritual person is able to judge a person ruled by the Spirit of God.

| 2.16 TEV | RSV |
|---|---|
| As the scripture says, "Who knows the mind of the Lord? Who is able to give him advice?" We, however, have the mind of Christ. | "For who has known the mind of the Lord so as to instruct him?" But we have the mind of Christ. |

In support of his statement that the true nature, or worth, of a spiritual person cannot be assessed by an unspiritual person, Paul quotes Isaiah 40.13 in a form nearer to that found in the ancient Greek version, the Septuagint, than in the Hebrew text. The questions are rhetorical: the implied answers, in both cases, are negative: "No one knows the mind (that is, the thinking) of the Lord. No human being can give him advice." Here Lord is probably meant to refer to God, as in the Old Testament context.

**We**: this probably refers to Paul and his colleagues, those who proclaim the gospel.

    We have the mind of Christ: "We understand how Christ thinks," "Our
thinking is patterned after (or, controlled by) Christ's way of thinking." This is said in order to confirm the statement that the person who
has the Spirit is able to judge the value of everything (verse 15a).

# Chapter 3

Servants of God: "The Apostles Are God's Servants."
In the previous section Paul had written about those who are
spiritually mature (2.6), who are ruled by the Spirit of God (2.13,15).
In this section (3.1-23) he begins by pointing out to his readers that
they are not yet mature Christians, as shown by the factions and rivalries among them (3.1-4). This leads him to write specifically about the
part that he and Apollos had in the work in Corinth (3.5-9a) and in
more general terms about the work that all Christian leaders perform
(3.9b-15). The section ends (3.16-23) with warnings and assurances.

If this section seems too long, a natural break is provided at 3.16,
where a new section (3.16-23) can begin.

| 3.1 TEV | RSV |
|---|---|
| As a matter of fact, my broth-ers, I could not talk to you as I talk to people who have the Spirit; I had to talk to you as though you belonged to this world, as chil-dren in the Christian faith. | But I, brethren, could not address you as spiritual men, but as men of the flesh, as babes in Christ. |

As a matter of fact: "And I, on my part."
my brothers: see 1.10.
talk to you: here in the sense of "teach," "exhort," "instruct"
(in the Christian faith).
people who have the Spirit: as in 2.13,15.
you belonged to this world: this translates the Greek adjective
"carnal, fleshly" (see RSV "men of the flesh"). Paul doesn't say that
they were of this world, but that they acted as though they were; they
were still ruled by worldly aims, worldly desires; "as though you are
still controlled by worldly (or, ungodly) desires."
children in the Christian faith: "immature in your understanding of
the Christian faith" or "beginners..." or "like babies in your understanding."

| 3.2 TEV | RSV |
|---|---|
| I had to feed you milk, not solid food, because you were not ready for it. And even now you are not ready for it, | I fed you with milk, not solid food; for you were not ready for it; and even yet you are not ready, |

Paul continues the figure of children.
you were not ready for it: or "you had not grown enough to be able
to eat solid food, so I had to give you milk." Here solid food is a
figure of the more complex matters, matters requiring greater understanding, while milk stands for simple matters, more easily digested.

[ 26 ]

If the metaphors cannot be used: "I had to teach you simple spiritual truths, not deep and difficult ones, because...."

3.3

| TEV | RSV |
|---|---|
| because you still live as the people of this world live. When there is jealousy among you and you quarrel with one another, doesn't this prove that you belong to this world, living by its standards? | for you are still of the flesh. For while there is jealousy and strife among you, are you not of the flesh, and behaving like ordinary men? |

still live as the people of this world live: this translates the adjective "fleshly, carnal" (see RSV "of the flesh"), though it is not precisely the same Greek word as in verse 1.

Instead of the question form, When there is...doesn't this prove ...? of TEV, a statement may be used: "There is jealousy among you and you quarrel with one another. This proves...."

there is jealousy among you: "you are jealous (or, envious) of one another."

living by its standards: this translates the Greek "acting like (ordinary) people," "acting like people who are not Christians," "acting like people who don't know God."

Textual Note: some Greek manuscripts add "divisions" (after "jealousy...quarrel"), but this added word is not part of the original text.

3.4

| TEV | RSV |
|---|---|
| When one of you says, "I follow Paul," and another, "I follow Apollos"—aren't you acting like worldly people? | For when one says, "I belong to Paul," and another, "I belong to Apollos," are you not merely men? |

I follow Paul...I follow Apollos: see 1.12.

acting like worldly people: an expression synonymous with "acting like ordinary people" of the preceding verse.

This verse also may be represented as a statement of fact: "one of you says, 'I follow Paul,' and another says, 'I follow Apollos.' You are acting like worldly people."

Although the Greek text uses the singular, one and another, Paul is not talking just of two individuals but of two groups; so it may be better to translate "Some of you...others," or "One group says...another group says."

3.5

| TEV | RSV |
|---|---|
| After all, who is Apollos? And who is Paul? We are simply God's servants, by whom you were led to believe. Each one of us does the work which the Lord gave him to do: | What then is Apollos? What is Paul? Servants through whom you believed, as the Lord assigned to each. |

who is...?: this question, repeated, is a rhetorical question and may be represented by a statement: "But Paul and Apollos are only God's servants...." Paul speaks of himself in the third person, and it may be necessary to say "I, Paul."

to believe: if an object is needed it could be "God" or "Jesus Christ" or "the gospel." Probably "Jesus Christ" is intended.

the Lord: here it probably refers to God, although it could be Jesus Christ.

| 3.6 TEV | RSV |
|---|---|
| I planted the seed, Apollos watered the plant, but it was God who made the plant grow. | I planted, Apollos watered, but God gave the growth. |

Here Paul uses the figure of a plant, or a crop, in speaking of the work that he and Apollos had done in Corinth.

watered the plant: or "watered the soil where the seed was planted." It may be necessary to use similes in place of metaphors: "My work among you was like that of a man who plants a seed, and Apollos' work was like that of a man who waters the soil (or, the plant)." In the case of what God does, however, a simile is not appropriate, since both in the figure of a plant and in the real matter of the church in Corinth, God is the one who causes growth. In some settings the agricultural language may not be easily understood, and so the translation can say "I began the work, Apollos continued it, but it was God who made it succeed (or, prosper)."

| 3.7 TEV | RSV |
|---|---|
| The one who plants and the one who waters really do not matter. It is God who matters, because he makes the plant grow. | So neither he who plants nor he who waters is anything, but only God who gives the growth. |

really do not matter: their work is, of course, important, but the really vital thing is to supply life and growth, which no person can do; only God can do that. Compared to what God does, the work that people do is quite unimportant.

The one...and the one...It is God: this can be stated in terms of the work done and not of the one doing the work: "The work done by the one who plants and the work done by the one who waters are not very important. It is the work done by God that is really important."

| 3.8 TEV | RSV |
|---|---|
| There is no difference between the man who plants and the man who waters; God will reward each one according to the work he has done. | He who plants and he who waters are equal, and each shall receive his wages according to his labor. |

There is no difference: this translates "(the two) are one" (see
RSV "are equal"). What is meant is that the importance of the work of
one is the same as that of the other. Any difference in the reward that
God will give them will be on the basis of the faithfulness with which
they did the work.

will reward: or "will pay," "will recompense."


3.9      TEV                                            RSV
For we are partners working together   For we are God's fellow workers;
for God, and you are God's field.      you are God's field, God's build-
   You are also God's building.        ing.


we: that is, Apollos and Paul, and therefore exclusive.

are partners working together for God: this translates "we are God's
fellow workers" (see RSV). This could mean "God's partners in the work,"
but more probably (in light of what Paul says in verse 5) it means "we
are partners who together work for God," "fellow workers in God's service."

TEV separates the next statement ("You are God's building") and
begins a paragraph with it because the figure changes from plant to
building.

You are also God's building: "You are also a building that belongs
to (or, is built by) God." If a simile is necessary: "You are also like
a building that belongs to (or, is built by) God."


3.10     TEV                                            RSV
Using the gift that God gave me,          According to the grace of God
I did the work of an expert builder    given to me, like a skilled master
and laid the foundation, and an-       builder I laid a foundation, and
other man is building on it. But       another man is building upon it.
each one must be careful how he        Let each man take care how he
builds.                                builds upon it.


the gift: "the skill," "the ability," "the capacity." This translates the Greek word usually translated "grace" (see 1.4).

an expert builder: "a skilled architect."

how he builds: "the kind of building he puts up (or, constructs)."

It may be necessary to use similes, as follows: "My work (among
you) was like the work of a skilled architect, who lays the foundation.
Another man's work is like that of a builder, who constructs a building
on the foundation."


3.11     TEV                                            RSV
For God has already placed Jesus       For no other foundation can any
Christ as the one and only foun-       one lay than that which is laid,
dation, and no other foundation can    which is Jesus Christ.
be laid.


Paul's warning is based on the fact that even though he himself
had laid the particular foundation of the Christian work in Corinth,

3.11

there is only one foundation on which a church can be built: the foundation laid by God. Jesus Christ is the only foundation—there is no other, and this is the very foundation that Paul laid in Corinth.

| 3.12 TEV | RSV |
|---|---|
| Some will use gold or silver or precious stones in building on the foundation; others will use wood or grass or straw. | Now if any one builds on the foundation with gold, silver, precious stones, wood, hay, straw— |

Still using figurative language, Paul talks about the quality of the material which different builders will use. Some materials are expensive and durable, like gold or silver or precious stones; other materials are cheap and wear out quickly, like wood or grass or straw.

| 3.13 TEV | RSV |
|---|---|
| And the quality of each person's work will be seen when the Day of Christ exposes it. For on that Day fire will reveal everyone's work; the fire will test it and show its real quality. | each man's work will become manifest; for the Day will disclose it, because it will be revealed with fire, and the fire will test what sort of work each one has done. |

will be seen: "will be revealed," "will be known," "will appear."
fire: this is the fire of judgment, which is associated with the Day of Christ (see 1.8).
will test it and show its real quality: this translates one Greek verb, "to put to the test," "to prove," "to determine the quality (or, value) of." "On that Day there will be the fire of judgment, and by means of that fire everyone's work will be tested and its real quality will be shown."

| 3.14 TEV | RSV |
|---|---|
| If what was built on the foundation survives the fire, the builder will receive a reward. | If the work which any man has built on the foundation survives, he will receive a reward. |

The whole verse may be restructured: "God will reward the person whose construction (or, work) survives the fire (or, is not destroyed by the fire)."

| 3.15 TEV | RSV |
|---|---|
| But if anyone's work is burnt up, then he will lose it; but he himself will be saved, as if he had escaped through the fire. | If any man's work is burned up, he will suffer loss, though he himself will be saved, but only as through fire. |

is burnt up: "is destroyed by the fire (of God's judgment)."

he will lose it: or "he will not get a reward."
he himself will be saved: "he will not be destroyed (by the fire)."
as if he had escaped through the fire: this is a vivid image of a
man who barely escapes with his life from a burning building.


| 3.16 | TEV | RSV |
|---|---|---|
| | Surely you know that you are God's temple and that God's Spirit lives in you! | Do you not know that you are God's temple and that God's Spirit dwells in you? |

Here Paul goes on to another figure, from that of a building to
that of a temple, or sanctuary. No longer does Paul speak of the work
that he and Apollos have done but only of the responsibility of the
Corinthian Christians themselves. If a new section is begun here (end-
ing at 3.23) its heading can be "The Christian Life" or "The Holiness
of the Church."
This verse is in the form of a question (see RSV) which may be
represented as a statement (TEV).
you are God's temple: "you are a temple that belongs to God." Paul
is speaking to the people in collective terms: they, the Corinthian
Church, are a temple of God, the temple owned by God, the temple where
God is truly worshiped. Or a simile may be used: "You are like a temple
in which God is worshiped."
God's Spirit lives in you: this applies both individually and
collectively to individual Christians and to the Church.


| 3.17 | TEV | RSV |
|---|---|---|
| | So if anyone destroys God's temple, God will destroy him. For God's temple is holy, and you yourselves are his temple. | If any one destroys God's temple, God will destroy him. For God's temple is holy, and that temple you are. |

destroys: or "profanes," "corrupts." But the application of the
same verb to a person makes the meaning destroys more appropriate. By
their factions and quarrels the Corinthian Christians were destroying
the church, God's temple.
For holy, see 1.2.


| 3.18 | TEV | RSV |
|---|---|---|
| | No one should fool himself. If anyone among you thinks that he is wise by this world's stand-ards, he should become a fool, in order to be really wise. | Let no one deceive himself. If any one among you thinks that he is wise in this age, let him become a fool that he may become wise. |

fool himself: "deceive himself," "believe what isn't true."
by this world's standards: this translates the phrase "in this
age"; see in 1.20 the discussion of the Greek word for "age."
become a fool: that is, by this world's standards. Here Paul is

again contrasting the true wisdom, that of God and Christ, and the false wisdom, the wisdom of this "age."

| 3.19 TEV | RSV |
|---|---|
| For what this world considers to be wisdom is nonsense in God's sight. As the scripture says, "God traps the wise in their cleverness"; | For the wisdom of this world is folly with God. For it is written, "He catches the wise in their craftiness," |

what this world considers to be wisdom: "what people of this world (or, age) think is wise."
is nonsense in God's sight: "God considers to be nonsense (or, foolishness)."
the scripture: Paul quotes Job 5.13.
God traps the wise in their cleverness: this is a figure of catching in a snare or trap as one catches wild animals or birds. God uses the cleverness of the wise to catch them, a figure of God's judgment on them.

| 3.20 TEV | RSV |
|---|---|
| and another scripture says, "The Lord knows that the thoughts of the wise are worthless." | and again, "The Lord knows that the thoughts of the wise are futile." |

another scripture: here Paul quotes Psalm 94.11.
The Lord: God.
are worthless: "are futile," "mean nothing," "are useless."

| 3.21 TEV | RSV |
|---|---|
| No one, then, should boast about what men can do. Actually everything belongs to you: | So let no one boast of men. For all things are yours, |

This warning matches the scripture quoted in 1.31.
what men can do: "human accomplishments," "human deeds." Or else the Greek may be taken to mean, "No one should boast about men (or, human beings)"—a direct reference to Apollos, Peter, and Paul.
everything belongs to you: as verse 22 makes clear, Paul is saying that the Corinthian Christians, as a church, are masters, not subjects. The leaders they had were God's gift to the church; the Corinthian Christians don't owe allegiance to Paul, or to Apollos, or to Peter. Instead, these leaders owe their allegiance to the Corinthian church. In the same way all issues of life and death, all opportunities of the present and the future, are all put at the disposal of the Church because the Church is subservient to Christ, who is subservient to God. So the Corinthian Christians must not be partisan in their allegiance and boast of any one man as though he were of greater value or had greater authority than someone else.

It may be difficult to say belongs to you in terms of what follows:
perhaps, "is at your disposal," "is for your benefit."

<table>
<tr><td>3.22-23    TEV</td><td>RSV</td></tr>
</table>

| 3.22-23    TEV | RSV |
|---|---|
| Paul, Apollos, and Peter; this world, life and death, the present and the future—all these are yours, 23 and you belong to Christ, and Christ belongs to God. | whether Paul or Apollos or Cephas or the world or life or death or the present or the future, all are yours; 23 and you are Christ's; and Christ is God's. |

The list divides naturally into three classes: (1) persons: Paul,
Apollos, Peter: they work for you, they serve you; (2) this world: all
it offers; nothing that belongs to this world is to be your master; (3)
all of life and even death are not your masters; all that the present
offers and also all that the future will bring—all these are yours.
    Paul is able to make this extraordinary statement about the
supremacy and sovereignty of the church because those who constitute the
church belong to Christ and are subject to him, as Christ belongs to
God—who alone is supreme and sovereign over all.

# Chapter 4

Apostles of Christ: "The Work of the Apostles."
In this section (4.1-21) Paul discourses at length upon his activity in the church at Corinth. He defends himself from what seems to have been sharp criticism of his work, and in vivid language (verses 9-13) describes the position occupied by himself and his colleagues as the lowest possible. But he is sending Timothy to Corinth (verse 17) and looks forward to his own visit there (verses 19-21).

| 4.1 | TEV | RSV |
|---|---|---|
| | You should think of us as Christ's servants, who have been put in charge of God's secret truths. | This is how one should regard us, as servants of Christ and stewards of the mysteries of God. |

You should think of us: this translates the Greek indefinite agent "One should think of us" (compare RSV). This could be represented by "Everyone should consider us" or "...regard us."

us: this refers to Paul and his colleagues.

Christ's servants: this translates a different word from the one used in 3.5, but the meaning is the same. Some translations try to maintain a distinction, saying here "subordinates, helpers, underlings," but most translations use the same word.

who have been put in charge of: this translates the Greek noun for "stewards" (RSV). (The Greek text has "servants of Christ and stewards of God's mysteries," but Paul is not saying that these are two separate and different offices; so TEV Christ's servants, who.) In Luke 16.1-3 TEV translates the same Greek noun by manager (and in 1 Cor 9.17 the related noun is translated [this] task). The word describes the office of a person in charge of some matter, who is directly responsible to his superior. So a noun like "administrator" or "manager" may be used, or else an expression like "have the responsibility of," "have been given the task."

secret truths: these are truths which were not known in the past but have now been revealed in the gospel (see 2.1). The Greek phrase "stewards of God's mysteries" (see RSV) means "those who have been given the task (or, responsibility) of proclaiming (or, making known) God's secret truths."

| 4.2 | TEV | RSV |
|---|---|---|
| | The one thing required of such a servant is that he be faithful to his master. | Moreover it is required of stewards that they be found trustworthy. |

The one thing: "The main quality," "The most important quality."
of such a servant: "of stewards," "of managers," "of administrators."

he be faithful to his master: "he be trustworthy," "he be reliable
(or, dependable)," "he do his job faithfully."


4.3          TEV                                    RSV
Now, I am not at all concerned        But with me it is a very small
about being judged by you or by       thing that I should be judged by
any human standard; I don't even      you or by any human court. I do
pass judgment on myself.              not even judge myself.

Paul here is emphatic: "As for me, it is absolutely of no importance." He emphasizes in verses 3-6 that the Lord, who appointed him to
his task, is the only one to judge him.
   any human standard: literally "any human court." This can be com-
bined with what precedes, as follows: "I am not at all concerned about
being judged by you or by anyone else."


4.4          TEV                                    RSV
My conscience is clear, but that      I am not aware of anything against
does not prove that I am really       myself, but I am not thereby
innocent. The Lord is the one who     acquitted. It is the Lord who
passes judgment on me.                judges me.

   My conscience is clear: "My own conscience does not accuse me,"
"I myself am not aware of any wrong I have done."
   but that does not prove that I am really innocent: the context is
still Paul's faithfulness as a steward, and in this respect he claims
that his clear conscience is not final and complete proof of his faithfulness. Paul is not talking about any kind of sin as such, nor is he
claiming that he doesn't know of any sin that he has committed.
   The Lord: probably Jesus Christ.
   is the one who passes judgment on me: "is the one who will judge
me," "is my judge."


4.5          TEV                                    RSV
So you should not pass judgment       Therefore do not pronounce judg-
on anyone before the right time       ment before the time, before the
comes. Final judgment must wait       Lord comes, who will bring to
until the Lord comes; he will         light the things now hidden in
bring to light the dark secrets       darkness and will disclose the
and expose the hidden purposes of     purposes of the heart. Then every
people's minds. And then every-       man will receive his commendation
one will receive from God the         from God.
praise he deserves.

   Paul here warns his critics in the Corinthian Church that the only
one capable of passing complete judgment is the Lord himself, and this

will not take place until the end. Human beings are not to try to do what only the Lord himself does.

until the Lord comes: this refers to the Day of Judgment (see 1.8), when Jesus Christ will judge all people. At that time final judgment will be made.

the hidden purposes of people's minds: "the designs (or, thoughts) of human hearts," "people's secret intentions (or, desires)." These remain hidden from human sight, and only the Lord can expose them.

will receive from God the praise he deserves: "God will praise each person as that person deserves."

| 4.6 | TEV | RSV |
|---|---|---|

| TEV | RSV |
|---|---|
| For your sake, my brothers, I have applied all this to Apollos and me, using the two of us as an example, so that you may learn what the saying means, "Observe the proper rules." None of you should be proud of one person and despise another. | I have applied all this to myself and Apollos for your benefit, brethren, that you may learn by us not to go beyond what is written, that none of you may be puffed up in favor of one against another. |

For your sake: "So that you will understand what I am talking about." my brothers: see 1.10.

I have applied all this to Apollos and me: "I have used Apollos and myself as an example in all that I have written on the subject." Paul is saying that his comments on the work Apollos and he had done in Corinth (3.4-9a) are a particular example of the general statements he has just made (4.1-5) about the responsibility of stewards of God's secret truths.

you may learn what the saying means, "Observe the proper rules": this is a very difficult passage in Greek to understand and there is no certainty as to what it means. One outstanding scholar and translator, James Moffatt, leaves the words untranslated, saying in a footnote that "The text and meaning of the phrase...are beyond recovery." And the *Traduction oecuménique de la Bible* likewise refuses to translate. Literally the words seem to say "that in us you may learn (the meaning of) 'Not beyond (or, above) what is written.'" (Some late Greek manuscripts added a verb at the end, thus changing the meaning to "that in us you may learn not to think beyond [or, above] what is written." See KJV.) TEV translates "in us" by using the two of us as an example. In attempting to decide the meaning of the text as it now stands, the biggest problem is to determine what the phrase "what is written" means in this context. Normally the Greek phrase means "the Scriptures," and this is the meaning given by many translations, either "what the Scriptures say (or, determine)" or else "what God has decided." So some will translate "...you may learn that it is forbidden to go beyond what the Scriptures say" or "...what God has determined." But the Greek phrase may be understood to mean rules in general; so TEV the proper rules. If the phrase refers to the (Hebrew) Scriptures, there is no way of knowing what particular passage Paul is talking about. Some take "what is written" to refer to the terms of a contract; but such a reference is, at best, obscure. Either "the Scriptures" or "the rules" seems the best choice a translator has.

be proud of: "be puffed up (with pride)."
be proud of one person and despise another: "favor one person over another," "esteem one person more highly than another."

| 4.7 | TEV | RSV |
|---|---|---|

Who made you superior to others? Didn't God give you everything you have? Well, then, how can you boast, as if what you have were not a gift?

For who sees anything different in you? What have you that you did not receive? If then you received it, why do you boast as if it were not a gift?

Who made you: logically, you should refer to the person who esteems one person more highly. But Paul is now talking directly to the person (you is singular) who thinks himself superior to someone else. He goes from the object of pride to the person who is proud.

Who made you superior to others?: "Who makes you so important?" This meaning seems preferable to RSV "For who sees anything different in you?" The question is ironical: Paul is denying, in fact, that such a person is really superior.

Didn't God give you everything you have?: this translates the Greek "What do you have that you did not receive?" Any qualification or skill is God's gift, as the next question makes clear.

Well, then, how can you boast...?: "Since what you have is God's gift, you have no right to boast," "You have no right to boast, for what you have was given you by God."

| 4.8 | TEV | RSV |
|---|---|---|

Do you already have everything you need? Are you already rich? Have you become kings, even though we are not? Well, I wish you really were kings, so that we could be kings together with you.

Already you are filled! Already you have become rich! Without us you have become kings! And would that you did reign, so that we might share the rule with you!

you: here Paul uses the plural; he no longer addresses just one person but all those in the Corinthian church who shared that attitude. These would be particularly the leaders of the local factions; it does not seem that Paul would condemn in such strong terms all the Corinthian Christians.

Some editions of the Greek text punctuate as a question (so TEV), others as a statement (RSV). As a statement, it is ironical: "You think you have everything you need!" The same is true of the next two questions; compare TEV and RSV.

Have you become kings, even though we are not?: "Are you ruling (as kings) without (or, apart from) us?" It is difficult to determine exactly the force of the Greek verb "to rule as king." It may be taken in a general sense (as TEV has it) of being in command, of having complete authority, but there may be a reference here to the Kingdom of God, so that the meaning is "You are acting as though the Kingdom of God has fully arrived."

we: Paul and his colleagues.

<u>I wish you really were kings</u>...: "I wish you were ruling, so that we rule with you" or "...so that we might share in your rule."

4.9        TEV

For it seems to me that God has given the very last place to us apostles, like men condemned to die in public as a spectacle for the whole world of angels and of mankind.

RSV

For I think that God has exhibited us apostles as last of all, like men sentenced to death; because we have become a spectacle to the world, to angels and to men.

<u>to us apostles</u>: Paul and his colleagues. Here <u>apostles</u> is not limited to the twelve disciples of Jesus but includes <u>Paul</u> and others who have been sent out by Christ to proclaim the gospel.

<u>like men condemned to die in public as a spectacle</u>: the language seems to be drawn from the public shows where <u>condemned</u> criminals were placed in an arena to be killed by wild animals.

<u>the whole world of angels and of mankind</u>: "for the whole world to see, including angels and mankind." The "arena" is filled with all living beings, angelic and human.

4.10        TEV

For Christ's sake we are fools; but you are wise in union with Christ! We are weak, but you are strong! We are despised, but you are honored!

RSV

We are fools for Christ's sake, but you are wise in Christ. We are weak, but you are strong. You are held in honor, but we in disrepute.

Paul again uses irony as he compares the status of the apostles and of those arrogant leaders in the Corinthian church.

4.11        TEV

To this very moment we go hungry and thirsty; we are clothed in rags; we are beaten; we wander from place to place;

RSV

To the present hour we hunger and thirst, we are ill-clad and buffeted and homeless,

<u>clothed in rags</u>: "poorly clothed," "lack proper clothing."

<u>we wander from place to place</u>: "we are homeless," "we have no homes."

4.12        TEV

we wear ourselves out with hard work. When we are cursed, we bless; when we are persecuted, we endure;

RSV

and we labor, working with our own hands. When reviled, we bless; when persecuted, we endure;

we wear ourselves out with hard work: "we work hard to make a living," "we support ourselves by hard manual labor."

When we are cursed, we bless: "When others curse (or, insult) us, we bless them (or, wish them well)."


4.13     TEV

when we are insulted, we answer back with kind words. We are no more than this world's garbage; we are the scum of the earth to this very moment!

RSV

when slandered, we try to conciliate; we have become, and are now, as the refuse of the world, the offscouring of all things.

garbage: "rubbish," "refuse," "trash."
the scum of the earth: this is a common metaphor in English, and in this context means the same as garbage. RSV "offscouring" is the dirt and grime that is scoured off (that is, washed or scrubbed off) dishes and pots. Another figurative expression in English, used by some translations, is "the dregs of humanity." Most languages have appropriate equivalents to describe people who are thought of as absolutely worthless.


4.14     TEV

I write this to you, not because I want to make you feel ashamed, but to instruct you as my own dear children.

RSV

I do not write this to make you ashamed, but to admonish you as my beloved children.

Paul explains his purpose in making these bitter accusations.
to you: this seems to include all Corinthian Christians.
instruct: "admonish" (RSV), "teach a lesson to," "make you understand."
as my own dear children: "as though you were my dear children" or "...my children, whom I love."


4.15     TEV

For even if you have ten thousand guardians in your Christian life, you have only one father. For in your life in union with Christ Jesus I have become your father by bringing the Good News to you.

RSV

For though you have countless guides in Christ, you do not have many fathers. For I became your father in Christ Jesus through the gospel.

Here Paul justifies his calling the Corinthian Christians my own dear children.
guardians: "guides," "instructors," "teachers," that is, in the Christian faith. The Greek word was used to refer to a slave who took the children to school and who also looked after them when they were not in school. In a more general sense it referred to an instructor, a teacher.

you have only one father: literally "you don't have many fathers" (see RSV). Paul was the only spiritual father they had; he had proclaimed the gospel to them and had thus become their father. "I am like a father to you because you became Christians as a result of my preaching the gospel to you."

| 4.16 | TEV | RSV |
|---|---|---|
| I beg you, then, to follow my example. | | I urge you, then, be imitators of me. |

to follow my example: "to do (or, think) as I do," "to imitate me." Children should follow the example of their father.

| 4.17 | TEV | RSV |
|---|---|---|
| For this purpose I am sending to you Timothy, who is my own dear and faithful son in the Christian life. He will remind you of the principles which I follow in the new life in union with Christ Jesus and which I teach in all the churches everywhere. | | Therefore I send$^g$ to you Timothy, my beloved and faithful child in the Lord, to remind you of my ways in Christ, as I teach them everywhere in every church. |

$^g$Or *am sending*

For this purpose: that is, to help them follow Paul's example.
Timothy: one of Paul's colleagues who traveled with him and helped in the work (Acts 19.22; Phil 2.19-22).
my own dear and faithful son in the Christian life: in the same sense that the Corinthian Christians were Paul's spiritual children. So a simile may be more appropriate; "who is like a dear son to me."
faithful: either to Paul or to the Lord. Probably the former is meant. Or else "trustworthy," "dependable."
the principles which I follow: literally "my paths"; or "my conduct," "my behavior," "the way I live."
the new life in union with Christ Jesus: see 1.2.
all the churches: Paul taught the same Christian principles in every church. He did not require of one group of Christians what he did not require of other groups.

| 4.18 | TEV | RSV |
|---|---|---|
| Some of you have become proud because you have thought that I would not be coming to visit you. | | Some are arrogant, as though I were not coming to you. |

In verses 18-21 Paul deals with his plan to visit the church soon, and a new section could be made here with the heading: "Paul's Plan to Visit the Corinthian Church."
have become proud: the same verb here that is used in verse 6.

The verse may be restructured: "Some of you think that I am not coming to visit you and so they have become proud (or, arrogant)."

| 4.19 TEV | RSV |
|---|---|
| If the Lord is willing, however, I will come to you soon, and then I will find out for myself the power which these proud people have, and not just what they say. | But I will come to you soon, if the Lord wills, and I will find out not the talk of these arrogant people but their power. |

the Lord: God.

the power: this is spiritual power, the power that is given by the Spirit of God; it is not physical strength or superior status.

the power...not just what they say: "whether these people can really do anything...or whether all they can do is talk."

| 4.20 TEV | RSV |
|---|---|
| For the Kingdom of God is not a matter of words but of power. | For the kingdom of God does not consist in talk but in power. |

the Kingdom of God is not a matter of: "does not consist in." God's rule in the lives of people does not show itself in words but in deeds, in actions. So the translation may say "When God rules over the life of a person, this is shown by that person's actions (or, by what that person does) and not by his words (or, and not by what he says)."

| 4.21 TEV | RSV |
|---|---|
| Which do you prefer? Shall I come to you with a whip, or in a spirit of love and gentleness? | What do you wish? Shall I come to you with a rod, or with love in a spirit of gentleness? |

with a whip: "to punish you." As their (spiritual) father Paul had the right to punish them.

# Chapter 5

Immorality in the Church: "Paul Condemns a Case of Immoral Conduct," "How the Church Must Deal with Immoral Behavior."

In this section (5.1-13) Paul discusses a serious matter: immoral conduct by one of the members of the church in Corinth; and he instructs the church how to deal with this matter (verses 1-5). Then he goes on to more general consideration of holy conduct as required of Christians by the sacrifice of Jesus Christ (verses 6-13).

5.1        TEV                      RSV

| TEV | RSV |
|---|---|
| Now, it is actually being said that there is sexual immorality among you so terrible that not even the heathen would be guilty of it. I am told that a man is sleeping with his stepmother! | It is actually reported that there is immorality among you, and of a kind that is not found even among pagans; for a man is living with his father's wife. |

Now: this is a transition marker; it shows that a new subject is beginning.

it is actually being said: "I have actually been told (or, heard)," "someone has actually told me." As in the similar instance in 1.11, there is no clear indication how the news reached Paul.

the heathen: "pagans," "non-Christians," "people who don't worship God."

is sleeping with: the Greek verb "to have" implies an illicit relationship; "is living with her as though she were his wife." Both Roman law and the Hebrew Scriptures (Lev 18.8; 20.11) prohibited marriage between a man and his stepmother. It is assumed here that the man's father (the stepmother's husband) is dead.

his stepmother: this translates the Greek "his father's wife" (see RSV). But the translation should not be understood to mean that she is the man's own mother, as "his father's wife" could be taken to mean.

5.2        TEV                      RSV

| TEV | RSV |
|---|---|
| How, then, can you be proud? On the contrary, you should be filled with sadness, and the man who has done such a thing should be expelled from your fellowship. | And you are arrogant! Ought you not rather to mourn? Let him who has done this be removed from among you. |

be proud: this translates the same verb that is used in 4.6; see also 4.18-19.

be filled with sadness: "feel deep remorse," "mourn."

the man: this seems to imply that the man's stepmother was not a member of the church.

[ 42 ]

should be expelled from your fellowship: "must be sent away from the church." Here is the application of the Old Testament verse Paul cites at the end of this chapter.

| 5.3-4 TEV | RSV |
|---|---|
| And even though I am far away from you in body, still I am there with you in spirit; and as though I were there with you, I have in the name of our Lord Jesus already passed judgment on the man who has done this terrible thing. As you meet together, and I meet with you in my spirit, by the power of our Lord Jesus present with us, | For though absent in body I am present in spirit, and as if present, I have already pronounced judgment 4 in the name of the Lord Jesus on the man who has done such a thing. When you are assembled, and my spirit is present, with the power of our Lord Jesus, |

TEV combines the two verses, since it places in the name of our Lord Jesus (which begins verse 4) between I have and already passed judgment (which is at the end of verse 3; see RSV).

I am far away from you in body: "I am absent physically," "I am not present with you personally (or, in body)."

I am there with you in spirit: "In my thoughts I am with you," "in my heart I am present with you." Paul is not saying that his spirit has left his body in Ephesus and gone to Corinth. Care must be taken not to say or imply this in translation. In some cultures it is believed that a person's spirit can leave the person (usually while the person is asleep or in a trance) and go somewhere else; but Paul is not talking about this.

as though I were there with you: "just as if I were present with you in Corinth."

in the name of our Lord Jesus: "acting under the authority of our Lord Jesus," or "by the power of our Lord Jesus." This expression is synonymous with the one used in the next sentence.

our: inclusive.

and I meet with you in my spirit: "You are to act as though I were there present with you."

Textual Note: instead of our Lord Jesus, some Greek manuscripts have "the Lord Jesus"; others have "the Lord Jesus Christ," and a very large number have "our Lord Jesus Christ." Either "the Lord Jesus" or "our Lord Jesus" is to be preferred.

| 5.5 TEV | RSV |
|---|---|
| you are to hand this man over to Satan for his body to be destroyed, so that his spirit may be saved in the Day of the Lord. | you are to deliver this man to Satan for the destruction of the flesh, that his spirit may be saved in the day of the Lord Jesus.[h]<br><br>[h]Other ancient authorities omit *Jesus* |

[ 43 ]

to Satan: "to the authority (or, power) of Satan." Satan is the ruler of the forces of evil; the name (in Hebrew) means "the opponent" or "the accuser." The precise sense of Paul's command is not clear; the purpose of the action is that the man's body (Greek, "flesh") be destroyed. Paul's thinking seems to be that by expelling the man from the fellowship of the church he will be in the realm controlled by Satan, that is, the world, the realm of sickness and death, and so he will die, but his spirit will be saved. But this makes sense only on the supposition that such a death is different from the death that awaits all people, and it is probable that in the background of Paul's command is the belief that the world would end in that generation and Christians would not die (see 15.51-57).

Some take "flesh" here to mean sinful desires, or mortal human nature. But it is difficult to understand how Paul could have meant that the rule of Satan over that man would result in the destruction of his sinful desires. Here it would appear that "flesh" is synonymous with "body."

the Day of the Lord: see 1.8.

Verses 3-5 may be restructured as follows: "3 I am separated from you physically (or, in body), but spiritually (or, in my spirit) I am present with you. And since I am there with you in my spirit, I have already passed judgment on the man who has committed this sin. 4 I have done this by the authority (or, in the name) of our Lord Jesus. You are to gather together, and in my spirit I will be with you. The power of our Lord Jesus will be present with us. 5 This man must be handed over to the power of Satan for his body to be destroyed, in order that his spirit will be saved in the Day of the Lord Jesus."

| 5.6 | TEV | RSV |
|---|---|---|
| | It is not right for you to be proud! You know the saying, "A little bit of yeast makes the whole batch of dough rise." | Your boasting is not good. Do you not know that a little leaven leavens the whole lump? |

to be proud: "to boast." With such a terrible sin in their fellowship, the Corinthian Christians have no right to boast about their Christian life (verse 2).

You know the saying: or "You know that...." The Greek is in the form of a question (see RSV), but it is not a request for information. What follows seems to be a proverbial expression (like the one in English, "A rotten apple spoils the whole barrel [of apples]").

yeast: a substance (also known as leaven) which is added to flour to make the mass of dough rise before being baked; here, as elsewhere, yeast is a figure of sin which spreads and infects others. There are various ways of translating it: "that which causes the bread to swell (or, to rise)"; "that which makes the bread to be sour." In some languages the name is "beer foam," which is what is actually used in the making of bread.

| 5.7          TEV | RSV |
|---|---|
| You must remove the old yeast of sin so that you will be entirely pure. Then you will be like a new batch of dough without any yeast, as indeed I know you actually are. For our Passover Festival is ready, now that Christ, our Passover lamb, has been sacrificed. | Cleanse out the old leaven that you may be a new lump, as you really are unleavened. For Christ, our paschal lamb, has been sacrificed. |

the old yeast of sin: TEV has added of sin in order to show the figurative use of the expression (and see verse 8).

entirely pure: literally "without leaven (or, yeast)."

Passover Festival: or "Passover meal." Passover was the Jewish festival which celebrated the deliverance of the ancient Hebrews from their slavery in Egypt. As part of the festival, all leavened bread was discarded and only bread made without yeast was eaten during the following week (see Exo 12.14-20).

Paul uses this historical event as applying to the Church. The Church has been set free from bondage; it celebrates its Passover. And its Passover lamb is Jesus Christ, who was sacrificed. He is the "lamb" sacrificed for our salvation, just as in the Passover in Egypt each family sacrificed a lamb and smeared its blood on the door of the house, so that the Angel of Death would pass over that house and not kill the first born son inside. So as the Church celebrates its exodus from the realm of sin and death, it must not have any "yeast" of sin, but must be completely pure, like bread that has no yeast in it.

| 5.8          TEV | RSV |
|---|---|
| Let us celebrate our Passover, then, not with bread having the old yeast of sin and wickedness, but with the bread that has no yeast, the bread of purity and truth. | Let us, therefore, celebrate the festival, not with the old leaven, the leaven of malice and evil, but with the unleavened bread of sincerity and truth. |

the old yeast of sin and wickedness: or "the old yeast, which represents sin and evil."

the bread that has no yeast, the bread of purity and truth: "the unleavened bread, which represents purity and truth."

purity: or "sincerity," "honesty."

The order can be changed: "We must celebrate our Passover with purity (or, honesty) and truth, which are like bread without yeast. We must not have sin and wickedness, which are like bread made with yeast."

| 5.9          TEV | RSV |
|---|---|
| In the letter that I wrote you I told you not to associate with immoral people. | I wrote to you in my letter not to associate with immoral men; |

the letter that I wrote you: a letter written before this one but which has not been preserved (unless, as some think, part of it is 2 Cor 6.14—7.1).

not to associate with: "to have nothing to do with," "not make friends of," "have no fellowship with."

| 5.10 TEV | RSV |
|---|---|
| Now I did not mean pagans who are immoral or greedy or are theives, or who worship idols. To avoid them you would have to get out of the world completely. | not at all meaning the immoral of this world, or the greedy and robbers, or idolaters, since then you would need to go out of the world. |

pagans: "people who belong to this world"; see "age" in 1.20.
greedy: "want things that belong to others."
It is obviously impossible for the Corinthian Christians to avoid associating with sinful people as long as they, the Christians, are alive, living in this world.

| 5.11 TEV | RSV |
|---|---|
| What I meant was that you should not associate with a person who calls himself a brother but is immoral or greedy or worships idols or is a slanderer or a drunkard or a thief. Don't even sit down to eat with such a person. | But rather I wrote[i] to you not to associate with any one who bears the name of brother if he is guilty of immorality or greed, or is an idolater, reviler, drunkard, or robber—not even to eat with such a one. |

[i]Or now I write

What I meant was: or "What I mean is." As the RSV footnote shows, the Greek verb "I wrote" may be taken to mean "I write (in this letter)." So the translation may be, "Now I am writing you that...."

calls himself a brother: "says he is a Christian," "claims to be a Christian."

is a slanderer: "says evil things about others," "accuses others of being sinful." The assumption is that such accusation is false.

sit down to eat with: "have a meal with," "eat with."

| 5.12-13 TEV | RSV |
|---|---|
| After all, it is none of my business to judge outsiders. God will judge them. But should you not judge the members of your own fellowship? As the scripture says, "Remove the evil man from your group." | For what have I to do with judging outsiders? Is it not those inside the church whom you are to judge? 13 God judges those outside. "Drive out the wicked person from among you." |

TEV combines the two verses, since the statement "God will judge the outsiders" is in verse 13 (see RSV), while the question "Should you not judge the insiders?" is in verse 12 (see RSV); TEV has reversed the order of the two.

After all, it is none of my business: this translates a question (see RSV). Paul says that it is not his responsibility as a Christian to judge people who are not members of the church; that is God's responsibility.

should you not judge...?: the question is rhetorical, and the meaning may be represented by a statement: "you should judge (or, pass judgment on)...."

As the scripture says: these words are not in Greek, but what follows is a quotation of a saying found in Deuteronomy 17.7; 19.19; 22.21,24; 24.7. It is not necessary, however, in translation to say As the scripture says. But notice that RSV, by placing the words that follow within quotation marks, takes them to be a quotation.

Remove: "Expel," "Drive out." See verse 2.

# Chapter 6

Lawsuits against Fellow Christians: "How to Settle Differences among Christians."

Paul's mention of "outsiders" (in 5.12-13) leads him to discuss the matter of how differences among church members are to be settled. It is wrong for Christians to submit their disputes to secular courts; they should settle them within the fellowship of the church (6.1-6). Christians are to live a life completely different from that lived by people of the world; their new life in union with Christ has set them free from the old ways (6.7-11).

| 6.1 TEV | RSV |
|---|---|
| If one of you has a dispute with a fellow Christian, how dare he go before heathen judges instead of letting God's people settle the matter? | When one of you has a grievance against a brother, does he dare go to law before the unrighteous instead of the saints? |

a dispute: "a difference of opinion," "a legal matter," "a complaint."

a fellow Christian: "another member of the church."

how dare he...?: the question is rhetorical; it condemns the action. A statement may be preferable: "he must not go before heathen judges for them to settle the matter. Instead, he must ask God's people to settle it." It should be clear in translation that he refers to one of you (and not to a fellow Christian).

God's people: in the Greek, "saints." See holy people in 1.2.

| 6.2 TEV | RSV |
|---|---|
| Don't you know that God's people will judge the world? Well, then, if you are to judge the world, aren't you capable of judging small matters? | Do you not know that the saints will judge the world? And if the world is to be judged by you, are you incompetent to try trivial cases? |

Don't you know...?: this may be a genuine question; most likely it is rhetorical: "You know that...."

will judge the world: God's people will share Christ's triumph and will take part in the final judgment not only of people but also of angels (verse 3).

aren't you capable...?: "aren't you able...?" "aren't you competent ...?" Or, as a statement, "you certainly are capable...."

small matters: "unimportant matters," "trivial things."

6.3             TEV
Do you not know that we shall
judge the angels? How much more,
then, the things of this life!

RSV
Do you not know that we are to
judge angels? How much more,
matters pertaining to this life!

we: inclusive.
How much more, then: or, as a complete sentence, "How much more,
then, we should judge the things of this life."
the things of this life: "ordinary matters," "everyday matters."
The verse may be restructured as follows: "You know that we Christians
will judge the angels. So we should be all the more willing (or, able)
to judge ordinary matters."

6.4             TEV
If such matters come up, are you
going to take them to be settled
by people who have no standing
in the church?

RSV
If then you have such cases, why
do you lay them before those who
are least esteemed by the church?

If: or "When."
are you going to take them...?: or "you should not take them." TEV
and RSV translate the Greek text punctuated as a question; but it can be
punctuated as a statement, in which case the verb may be understood not
as a present indicative but as a present imperative: "take them to be
settled." This is what a few translations do, the meaning being "When
such matters come up, appoint (or, select) as judges people in the
church who have no standing (or, who are not highly thought of)." This
would be pure sarcasm on Paul's part. The other interpretation seems
preferable, and Paul is referring to pagan magistrates, who are looked
down upon by Christians so far as their spiritual and moral qualifica-
tions are concerned.

6.5             TEV
Shame on you! Surely there is at
least one wise person in your
fellowship who can settle a dispute
between fellow Christians.

RSV
I say this to your shame. Can it
be that there is no man among
you wise enough to decide between members of the brotherhood,

Shame on you!: "You ought to be ashamed!"
Surely there is: this translates what in Greek is a question (see
RSV).

6.6             TEV
Instead, one Christian goes to
court against another and lets
unbelievers judge the case!

RSV
but brother goes to law against
brother, and that before unbelievers?

As RSV shows, verse 6 is part of the same sentence (in the form of
a rhetorical question) with verse 5. It seems better to divide the verses

into two separate sentences. TEV is in the form of a sarcastic statement. But it can be stated otherwise: "A Christian should not go to court and ask unbelievers (or, non-Christian judges) to settle a dispute he has against a fellow Christian."

| 6.7 TEV | RSV |
|---|---|
| The very fact that you have legal disputes among yourselves shows that you have failed completely. Would it not be better for you to be wronged? Would it not be better for you to be robbed? | To have lawsuits at all with one another is defeat for you. Why not rather suffer wrong? Why not rather be defrauded? |

have legal disputes among yourselves: or "try to settle your differences by going to court."

you have failed completely: "you have abandoned Christian principles," "you are not acting like Christians."

Would it not be better...?: or "It would be better" (in both instances).

to be wronged: "to endure injustice," "to have others do you wrong."

to be robbed: "to allow others to get what is yours."

| 6.8 TEV | RSV |
|---|---|
| Instead, you yourselves wrong one another and rob one another, even your own brothers! | But you yourselves wrong and defraud, and that even your own brethren. |

Instead of patiently enduring wrong, they are actively promoting wrong among themselves.

rob: "steal from."

your own brothers: "your own fellow Christians."

| 6.9-10 TEV | RSV |
|---|---|
| Surely you know that the wicked will not possess God's Kingdom. Do not fool yourselves; people who are immoral or who worship idols or are adulterers or homosexual perverts 10 or who steal or are greedy or are drunkards or who slander others or are thieves—none of these will possess God's Kingdom. | Do you not know that the unrighteous will not inherit the kingdom of God? Do not be deceived; neither the immoral, nor idolaters, nor adulterers, nor sexual perverts, 10 nor thieves, nor the greedy, nor drunkards, nor revilers, nor robbers will inherit the kingdom of God. |

the wicked: "those who do wrong," "the wrongdoers" (as in verse 8, you...wrong one another).

possess: this translates the Greek "inherit" (RSV), which speaks of the blessings of the Kingdom of God as given by God to his people.

God's Kingdom: it is here used in the future sense, of God's blessings for his people in the life to come.

homosexual perverts: this translates two Greek nouns, "catamites (or, pathics)" and "sodomites," which characterize the two roles played in male homosexual relations, the passive and the active role. Most translations use one descriptive word or phrase for the two; some have two words, using "male prostitutes" (NIV) or "effeminate" (KJV) for the first one, and "homsexuals" or "sodomites" for the second one.

The list used by Paul reflects the conditions in Corinth. The city was known for its immorality, and a verb had been coined in Greek from the name of the city, "to corinthianize," that is, to lead an immoral life.

| 6.11 TEV | RSV |
|---|---|
| Some of you were like that. But you have been purified from sin; you have been dedicated to God; you have been put right with God by the Lord Jesus Christ and by the Spirit of our God. | And such were some of you. But you were washed, you were sanctified, you were justified in the name of the Lord Jesus Christ and in the Spirit of our God. |

you have been purified from sin: this translates the Greek "you have been washed" (see RSV). This may be a specific reference to baptism, but it would not do to translate "you have been baptized."

dedicated to God: "become God's (holy) people." See 1.2,30.

put right with God: see 1.30.

by the Lord Jesus Christ: this translates "in the name of the Lord Jesus Christ" (see RSV). Here TEV takes "name" to mean "power, authority."

our God: the our is inclusive; "the God we worship (or, serve)."

SECTION HEADING

Use Your Bodies for God's Glory: "Warning against Sexual Immorality." Here Paul takes up the specific matter of sexual immorality. Christians in Corinth would be subject to the temptation to follow current standards in their society, and Paul warns them that their bodies are not to be used to satisfy sexual desires but for God's glory. Since Christ has redeemed them, their bodies are temples of the Holy Spirit.

| 6.12 TEV | RSV |
|---|---|
| Someone will say, "I am allowed to do anything." Yes; but not everything is good for you. I could say that I am allowed to do anything, but I am not going to let anything make me its slave. | "All things are lawful for me," but not all things are helpful. "All things are lawful for me," but I will not be enslaved by anything. |

Here and in verse 13 TEV takes the language to be that of a de-
bate which Paul carries on against those who argue that there is
nothing inherently wrong with immorality. RSV reflects the same understanding of the text by placing some of the material within quotation
marks (see also 10.23).

Someone: this person would be a member of the church, and Paul is
arguing with him, disputing his statements. For the sake of argument
Paul lets the statement stand but shows in his answer that such points
of view are wrong.

"I am allowed to do anything": "Everything is lawful for me,"
"There is no law against anything I want to do."

is good for you: "will benefit you," "will be of help to you."

I could say that I am allowed to do anything: or, as an exact
repetition of the opening words of the verse, "Someone else will say, 'I
am allowed to do anything'"(see RSV).

I am not going to let anything make me its slave: this is Paul's
own reply to the preceding hypothetical statement. "I will not be controlled (or, ruled) by any desire," "Nothing will be my master." Paul is
speaking specifically of sexual desires and practices.

| 6.13 | TEV | RSV |
|---|---|---|
| | Someone else will say, "Food is for the stomach, and the stomach is for food." Yes; but God will put an end to both. The body is not to be used for sexual immorality, but to serve the Lord; and the Lord provides for the body. | "Food is meant for the stomach and the stomach for food"—and God will destroy both one and the other. The body is not meant for immorality, but for the Lord, and the Lord for the body. |

In speaking of food and stomach here, Paul is not changing the subject from sex to food; rather he is responding to the argument that the
satisfaction of sexual desire is no more immoral than the satisfaction
of hunger; having sex is like eating food.

put an end to both: "destroy the two," "do away with them both."
Paul has in mind the time of the end. Perhaps it might help to say  "but
some day God will destroy both."

The body is not to be used for sexual immorality: Paul is not saying
that all sexual activity is wrong; he is saying that immorality is wrong.

The body is: or "Our bodies are."

to serve the Lord: this translates what is literally "for the Lord."
It may be stated, "for the Lord's glory (or, honor)." Here the Lord is
Jesus Christ.

and the Lord provides for the body: this translates "and the Lord
(is) for the body," exactly matching the statement "the body (is) for
the Lord." But the sense is not the same: it can hardly be said that the
purpose of the Lord is to serve the body, as is the body's purpose to
serve the Lord. So the meaning may be represented by "the Lord controls
(or, is ruler of) our bodies," or "the Lord uses our bodies for his
service."

| 6.14 TEV | RSV |
|---|---|
| God raised the Lord from death, and he will also raise us by his power. | And God raised the Lord and will also raise us up by his power. |

This statement is made because the body is included in the resurrection, which is the greatest demonstration of the Lord's care for our bodies. Just as Jesus was raised bodily from death, so shall Christians be raised from death.

| 6.15 TEV | RSV |
|---|---|
| You know that your bodies are parts of the body of Christ. Shall I take a part of Christ's body and make it part of the body of a prostitute? Impossible! | Do you not know that your bodies are members of Christ? Shall I therefore take the members of Christ and make them members of a prostitute? Never! |

Paul continues the argument, disputing the assumption that one's body is at one's own disposal and one may do with it as one wishes.
You know that: a rhetorical question, "Do you not know...?" (RSV).
parts: "members," "limbs and organs." The Christian person is drawn into the closest relationship to Christ and becomes part of Christ's own body.
a part of Christ's body: "a member of Christ's body," "what belongs to Christ's body."
and make it part of the body of a prostitute?: this is said in light of what Paul says in the next verse: in sexual intercourse a man and a woman become one body.

| 6.16 TEV | RSV |
|---|---|
| Or perhaps you don't know that the man who joins his body to a prostitute becomes physically one with her? The scripture says quite plainly, "The two will become one body." | Do you not know that he who joins himself to a prostitute becomes one body with her? For, as it is written, "The two shall become one flesh." |

Or perhaps you don't know: or "Surely you know."
joins his body to a prostitute: "has sexual relations with a prostitute."
The scripture: Paul quotes from Genesis 2.24, which is "The two will become one flesh." Here TEV uses the word body, since the argument is about being one body; and the Hebrew word for "flesh" in this passage means "being" or "person." Sexual union joins a man and a woman into one corporal being.
Care must be taken in translation to avoid giving the impression that the scripture quoted from Genesis 2.24 referred to intercourse between a man and a prostitute. In the quotation, the two means a man and his wife. So it might be better here to say "A man and a woman become one body."

| | |
|---|---|
| 6.17 TEV | RSV |
| But he who joins himself to the Lord becomes spiritually one with him. | But he who is united to the Lord becomes one spirit with him. |

he who: "the person who."

spiritually one: "one spirit." The union with the Lord Jesus Christ is spiritual, not physical. Perhaps the relation between the two unions can be stated: "A man and a woman become one physical body" and "...becomes one spiritual body with him."

| | |
|---|---|
| 6.18 TEV | RSV |
| Avoid immorality. Any other sin a man commits does not affect his body; but the man who is guilty of sexual immorality sins against his own body. | Shun immorality. Every other sin which a man commits is outside the body; but the immoral man sins against his own body. |

Avoid: "Flee," "Have nothing to do with." Or else, "Do not be immoral" or "Do not commit immoral acts."

does not affect his body: this translates what is literally "is outside his body," meaning "does not involve his body."

| | |
|---|---|
| 6.19 TEV | RSV |
| Don't you know that your body is the temple of the Holy Spirit, who lives in you and who was given to you by God? You do not belong to yourselves but to God; | Do you not know that your body is a temple of the Holy Spirit within you, which you have from God? You are not your own; |

Don't you know...?: "Surely you know."

your body is the temple: here Paul is speaking of the human body. It may be necessary to use a simile: "your body is (or, your bodies are) like a temple for the Holy Spirit."

You do not belong to yourselves: TEV adds but to God, which is implicit, as the first part of verse 20 shows.

| | |
|---|---|
| 6.20 TEV | RSV |
| he bought you for a price. So use your bodies for God's glory. | you were bought with a price. So glorify God in your body. |

he bought you for a price: here Paul compares the Christian to a slave; as a slave owner has paid for his slaves, so God has paid the price for his people (see also 7.23). Paul does not say what the price was, but elsewhere it is the death of God's Son (see 1 Peter 1.18-19; Rev 5.9).

for God's glory: "to bring honor to God."
Textual Note: some Greek manuscripts add to the final sentence ("Glorify God with your body") the words "and with your spirit, which belong to God." These additional words are not part of the original text.

# Chapter 7

SECTION HEADING

Questions about Marriage: "Paul Teaches about Christian Marriage."
Now Paul begins to consider certain matters that the Christians in
Corinth had written him about. In this section (7.1-16) he discusses
Christian marriage, giving his own opinion on the matter and also
quoting the Lord's teaching on divorce (verses 10-11).

7.1

| TEV | RSV |
|---|---|
| Now, to deal with the matters you wrote about. <br> A man does well not to marry.*e* | Now concerning the matters about which you wrote. It is well for a man not to touch a woman. |

*e*A man does well not to marry; *or*
You say that a man does well not
to marry.

Now, to deal with: this translates the Greek preposition "around,
about," meaning here "concerning." It will recur four more times (7.25;
8.1; 12.1; 16.1), in each instance as a reference to a subject that the
Corinthian Christians had written about to Paul. It is possible that
the letter had been brought to Paul by members of Chloe's family (see
1.11), but this is not necessarily so.
to deal with: "to consider," "to examine," "to discuss."
A man does well not to marry: it is not certain whether these are
Paul's own words or whether they were in the letter written by the
Corinthians, and Paul is quoting them. If they were in the letter, they
probably would have been in the form of a question, "Is it all right for
a man not to marry?" The Greek verb is literally "to touch" (see
2 Cor 6.17); here the meaning is "to have physical contact with," that
is, sexual intercourse (see the use of "to touch" in Gen 20.6;
Prov 6.29). Perhaps the best way to translate it in this context is "A
man does well not to have anything to do with women," where it is quite
evident that the phrase "anything to do with" refers to sexual relations.
But since the question of "touching" a woman would be in terms of marriage (and not extramarital sex), the TEV translation can be followed;
or else, "It is good for a man to lead a celibate life."
The alternative interpretation, in the TEV footnote, is followed by
some translations. But the translation in the text seems preferable, in
light of what Paul says in verse 2.

7.2

| TEV | RSV |
|---|---|
| But because there is so much im-morality, every man should have his own wife, and every woman should have her own husband. | But because of the temptation to immorality, each man should have his own wife and each woman her own husband. |

there is so much immorality: Paul is referring to the low moral standards in Corinth and the danger they would be to Christians. So a translation like RSV may be preferable: "because of the temptation to immorality" or "because of the danger of immorality" or "to avoid committing immoral acts."

every man...every woman: or, combining the two, "all (Christian) men and women should marry." But the extended form of the text is more emphatic.

| 7.3 TEV | RSV |
|---|---|
| A man should fulfill his duty as a husband, and a woman should fulfill her duty as a wife, and each should satisfy the other's needs. | The husband should give to his wife her conjugal rights, and likewise the wife to her husband. |

In this verse Paul tells the Corinthian Christians that every Christian husband and every Christian wife must satisfy the sexual needs of the spouse.

| 7.4 TEV | RSV |
|---|---|
| A wife is not the master of her own body, but her husband is; in the same way a husband is not the master of his own body, but his wife is. | For the wife does not rule over her own body, but the husband does; likewise the husband does not rule over his own body, but the wife does. |

Here Paul goes beyond traditional Jewish teaching, which spoke only of the husband's authority over his wife's body; Paul says that a Christian wife has the same rights over her husband's body that he has over hers. Paul's language is clear and frank; both the husband and the wife are bound to respect the sexual needs of the partner.

| 7.5 TEV | RSV |
|---|---|
| Do not deny yourselves to each other, unless you first agree to do so for a while in order to spend your time in prayer; but then resume normal marital relations. In this way you will be kept from giving in to Satan's temptation because of your lack of self-control. | Do not refuse one another except perhaps by agreement for a season, that you may devote yourselves to prayer; but then come together again, lest Satan tempt you through lack of self-control. |

deny yourselves to each other: "withhold from each other," "abstain from sexual intercourse." The verb translated deny means "to steal, to rob."

unless: continence in the marriage relationship is to be practiced only if (1) there is agreement between husband and wife; (2) it is temporary; (3) its purpose is to dedicate more time to spiritual matters.

The last sentence may be restructured: "If you do this, Satan will not be able to make you sin because of your lack of self-control." Paul is warning them that unless the suspension of normal marital relations is temporary, one or the other would be tempted to seek satisfaction in an extramarital relation.

For Satan, see 5.5.

Textual Note: some late Greek manuscripts, instead of prayer, have "fasting and prayer"; this expanded wording is not in the original text.

| 7.6 TEV | RSV |
|---|---|
| I tell you this not as an order, but simply as a permission. | I say this by way of concession, not of command. |

this: a reference to verses 2-7, in which Paul speaks of the right and need of Christian men and women to marry.

The verse may be restructured: "I am not ordering you to do this (or, get married); I am only advising you to do so." It is clear that Paul sees the single life as preferable to the married life, but he is not trying to impose his own opinion on the Corinthian Christians.

| 7.7 TEV | RSV |
|---|---|
| Actually I would prefer that all of you were as I am; but each one has a special gift from God, one person this gift, another one that gift. | I wish that all were as I myself am. But each has his own special gift from God, one of one kind and one of another. |

all of you: this includes both men and women.

as I am: as the next verse makes clear, Paul is not married. It seems implied that he has never married and feels no need to get married, and that he is a bachelor by choice. He does not boast about it; his continence is a special gift from God, and Paul recognizes that God does not bestow the same gift on all; he recognizes also that his gift is not morally or spiritually superior to someone else's gift.

For special gift see 1.7.

| 7.8 TEV | RSV |
|---|---|
| Now, to the unmarried and to the widows I say that it would be better for you to continue to live alone as I do. | To the unmarried and the widows I say that it is well for them to remain single as I do. |

to the unmarried: this includes both men and women.

to the widows: Paul does not specifically mention widowers, but certainly he is not making an exception of them.

to live alone as I do: this translates "to live as I do." The implicit fact (which both RSV and TEV make explicit) is that Paul is not married.

7.9        TEV

But if you cannot restrain your desires, go ahead and marry —it is better to marry than to burn with passion.

                    RSV

But if they cannot exercise self-control, they should marry. For it is better to marry than to be aflame with passion.

restrain your desires: "control yourselves," "master your (sexual) passion."

go ahead and marry: "then get married," "you ought to (or, should) marry."

to burn with passion: "to burn with unsatisfied sexual desire."

7.10-11        TEV

For married people I have a command which is not my own but the Lord's: a wife must not leave her husband; 11 but if she does, she must remain single or else be reconciled to her husband; and a husband must not divorce his wife.

                    RSV

To the married I give charge, not I but the Lord, that the wife should not separate from her husband 11 (but if she does, let her remain single or else be reconciled to her husband)—and that the husband should not divorce his wife.

In speaking to Christian married people, Paul is able to cite a command given by the Lord Jesus: it is not his own opinion (which may be disregarded) but is the Lord's command and so must be obeyed (see Mark 10.2-9).

must not leave: Paul does not use the verb "divorce," which he uses only in connection with the husband's action (but in verse 13 he does use the verb "to divorce" with reference to the wife's action).

Before citing the Lord's command about a husband not divorcing his wife, Paul recommends that if a Christian woman leaves her husband she must either remain single or else she must come back to her husband. Presumably Paul would prefer the second option, but he does not explicitly say so. It might be better to restructure the Lord's command as follows: "A wife must not leave her husband, and a husband must not divorce his wife. (But if a woman does leave her husband, she must either remain single or else return to her husband.)"

7.12        TEV

To the others I say (I, my-self, not the Lord): if a Christian man has a wife who is an unbeliever and she agrees to go on living with him, he must not divorce her.

                    RSV

To the rest I say, not the Lord, that if any brother has a wife who is an unbeliever, and she consents to live with him, he should not divorce her.

To the others: Paul has spoken of married people, unmarried people, and widowed people; here he takes up specifically the case where one of the partners is not a Christian. It is reasonable to suppose that such situations had arisen because only one of the partners had become a Christian after marriage. Jewish law prohibited a Jew marrying a non-Jew, and it is quite likely that in the same way a Christian was not supposed to marry a non-Christian.

(I, myself, not the Lord): Paul emphasizes that what follows is not a command from the Lord but his own opinion on the subject.

a Christian man: this translates "a brother" (see RSV).

if a Christian man has a wife who: this could possibly be understood to mean one of the man's wives, one who was not a Christian. To avoid this misunderstanding the translation may be "If a Christian man is married to a woman who is not a Christian" or "If the wife of a Christian man is not a Christian."

| 7.13 TEV | RSV |
|---|---|
| And if a Christian woman is married to a man who is an unbeliever and he agrees to go on living with her, she must not divorce him. | If any woman has a husband who is an unbeliever, and he consents to live with her, she should not divorce him. |

Exactly the same rule applies to a case where a Christian woman is married to a non-Christian man.

| 7.14 TEV | RSV |
|---|---|
| For the unbelieving husband is made acceptable to God by being united to his wife, and the unbelieving wife is made acceptable to God by being united to her Christian husband. If this were not so, their children would be like pagan children; but as it is, they are acceptable to God. | For the unbelieving husband is consecrated through his wife, and the unbelieving wife is consecrated through her husband. Otherwise, your children would be unclean, but as it is they are holy. |

Paul here states that the marriage between a Christian and a non-Christian is regarded by God as a holy union because one of the partners is a Christian.

is made acceptable to God: this translates the passive form of the verb "to be (or, make) holy." The basic concept is the Old Testament one of belonging to God's people (see 1.2,30). So the translation may be "belongs to God's people" or "belongs to God," "is dedicated to God."

by being united to his wife: or "because he is married to a Christian woman," "because his wife is a Christian."

If this were not so: that is, if it were not true that the Christian partner makes the marriage acceptable to God.

would be like pagan children: this translates "your children would be unclean" (RSV). The adjective "unclean" is here used in the Old Testament sense of that which is ceremonially impure, that is, not fit for God's service.

they are acceptable to God: the children are "holy" (just as the non-Christian spouse is "holy").

| 7.15 TEV | RSV |
|---|---|
| However, if the one who is not a believer wishes to leave the Christian partner, let it be so. In such cases the Christian partner, whether husband or wife, is free to act. God has called you to live in peace. | But if the unbelieving partner desires to separate, let it be so; in such a case the brother or sister is not bound. For God has called us$^l$ to peace.

$^l$Other ancient authorities read *you* |

Paul here says that the Christian spouse, whether husband or wife, should not try to keep the non-Christian spouse from leaving.

the Christian partner...is free to act: literally "is not bound," that is, is not constrained by Christian principles to try to maintain the marriage. Instead of free to act the translation could be "free to decide," "free to make a choice," "has the freedom to agree (to the non-Christian partner's decision to leave)." Or else the translation could be "is not bound by the marriage vows."

called: see 1.24.

you: as the RSV text and footnote show, some Greek manuscripts have "us"; if "us" is preferred, it is inclusive: "us Christians."

live in peace: God's call is not meant to force Christians to live a life of tension and conflict, in which a Christian is trying to maintain a marriage with an unwilling non-Christian partner.

| 7.16 TEV | RSV |
|---|---|
| How can you be sure, Christian wife, that you will not save$^f$ your husband? Or how can you be sure, Christian husband, that you will not save$^f$ your wife?

$^f$How can you be sure...that you will not save; *or* How do you know...that you will save. | Wife, how do you know whether you will save your husband? Husband, how do you know whether you will save your wife? |

As the TEV text and footnote show, it is not certain whether the implication of the question is that the Christian partner cannot save the non-Christian partner, or that the Christian partner can save the non-Christian partner. The question in the TEV text can be expressed as a statement: "You are not sure...that you will not save"; the question in the TEV footnote can be stated "You don't know (or, You are not sure) that you will save." In either case there is no assurance that what is seen as a possibility can actually be done.

Perhaps the form in the TEV footnote is preferable, since it follows Paul's recommendation that the Christian spouse, husband or wife, should not prevent the non-Christian spouse from leaving. Paul recommends this because the Christian partner, whether husband or wife, cannot be certain that he or she will be able to convert the non-Christian partner. If he or she were sure of it, then Paul would recommend that the Christian spouse not agree with the non-Christian's spouse's decision to leave.

save: here in terms of converting the partner to the Christian faith.

The verse may be restated as follows: "Christian wife, you cannot be sure that you can (or, will) save your husband; Christian husband, you cannot be sure that you can (or, will) save your wife."


SECTION HEADING

Live As God Called You: "Remain in the Condition (or, State) You Were in When God Called You."

In this section (7.17-24) Paul leaves off the matter of marriage and takes up specifically the racial (Jew or Gentile) and social (free or slave) condition of a person who has become a Christian. His advice is that no change in condition be attempted.


| 7.17 TEV | RSV |
|---|---|
| Each one should go on living according to the Lord's gift to him, and as he was when God called him. This is the rule I teach in all the churches. | Only, let every one lead the life which the Lord has assigned to him, and in which God has called him. This is my rule in all the churches. |

The verse in Greek begins with "except, nonetheless," which marks the beginning of a new subject. TEV has not reflected this in the text, but does so by beginning a new section. RSV has "Only." Perhaps: "However that may be," or "But to change the subject."

according to the Lord's gift to him: "according to what the Lord has given him (or, has decided his life should be)."

the Lord: probably Jesus Christ, in contrast with God in the following statement.

as he was: "in the condition (or, situation) he was in."

the rule I teach in all the churches: see the similar statement in 4.17.


| 7.18 TEV | RSV |
|---|---|
| If a circumcised man has accepted God's call, he should not try to remove the marks of circumcision; if an uncircumcised man has accepted God's call, he should not get circumcised. | Was any one at the time of his call already circumcised? Let him not seek to remove the marks of circumcision. Was any one at the time of his call uncircumcised? Let him not seek circumcision. |

Here Paul speaks of racial differences: Jews (circumcised) and Gentiles (uncircumcised).

The Greek text is in the form of a question (see RSV), which TEV
has represented by a statement.

circumcision: the rite of cutting off the foreskin of a Jewish
baby boy as a sign of God's covenant with the people of Israel (see Gen
17.9-14). Paul says that a Jewish man should not try to efface, or dis-
guise, the marks of his circumcision. That it was possible to do this
is seen by the account in 1 Maccabees 1.15.

| 7.19 TEV | RSV |
|---|---|
| For whether or not a man is circum- | For neither circumcision counts |
| cised means nothing; what matters | for anything nor uncircumcision, |
| is to obey God's commandments. | but keeping the commandments of |
| | God. |

This may be restated as follows: "It makes no difference (to God)
whether a man is circumcised or not. The important thing is to obey
God's commandments." Paul is saying that the presence or absence of
circumcision is without any spiritual value; in God's sight a circumcised man and an uncircumcised man are no different from each other.

| 7.20 TEV | RSV |
|---|---|
| Everyone should remain as he was | Every one should remain in the |
| when he accepted God's call. | state in which he was called. |

remain as he was: "not change his (racial or social) standing (or,
condition)" (see verses 8,11). Paul is not saying that no change at all
is required, nor that a person should continue with the same principles
of conduct and habits he had before he was converted. Paul is speaking
specifically of racial and social status.

| 7.21 TEV | RSV |
|---|---|
| Were you a slave when God called | Were you a slave when called? |
| you? Well, never mind; but if you | Never mind. But if you can gain |
| have a chance to become a free man, | your freedom, avail yourself of |
| use it.$^g$ | the opportunity.$^x$ |

$^g$but if you have a chance to become    $^x$Or *make use of your present*
a free man, use it; *or* but even if      *condition instead*
you have a chance to become a free
man, choose rather to make the
best of your condition as a slave.

never mind: "don't let that worry you."

As the TEV and RSV footnotes indicate, the Greek may be understood
to mean something quite different from the meaning that appears in the
text. In the passage in the text, Paul tells a Christian slave to become free, should he have the opportunity to do so; in the footnote he
tells him to remain a slave and make the best of his condition. The
majority of translations consulted follow the meaning expressed in the

text. Commentators also disagree on the matter, and a translator may choose to follow the alternative rendering in the footnote. In either case, it is advisable to give the alternative in a footnote.

| 7.22 | TEV | RSV |
|---|---|---|

**TEV**
For a slave who has been called by the Lord is the Lord's free man; in the same way a free man who has been called by Christ is his slave.

**RSV**
For he who was called in the Lord as a slave is a freedman of the Lord. Likewise he who was free when called is a slave of Christ.

Paul now speaks of physical and spiritual bondage and freedom: a person who is a slave when the Lord (that is, Jesus Christ) "calls" him becomes a free man—but a free man who belongs to the Lord, not one who is completely free from all control. The reverse is also true: a free man becomes Christ's slave when Christ calls him. For called see 1.24.

| 7.23 | TEV | RSV |
|---|---|---|

**TEV**
God bought you for a price; so do not become slaves of men.

**RSV**
You were bought with a price; do not become slaves of men.

God bought you for a price: this translates the passive "you were bought for a price" (see 6.20).

do not become slaves of men: here Paul seems to be talking about more than physical bondage. Christians should not be under the control of pagans, that is, adopt their principles and follow their practices.

| 7.24 | TEV | RSV |
|---|---|---|

**TEV**
My brothers, each one should remain in fellowship with God in the same condition that he was when he was called.

**RSV**
So, brethren, in whatever state each was called, there let him remain with God.

This is the final and summary statement: every Christian is to remain in the same racial or social condition he was in when he became a Christian.

My brothers: see 1.10.

in fellowship with God: "in the sight of God," "as God requires (or, wishes)."

SECTION HEADING

Questions about the Unmarried and the Widows: "Paul Teaches What Unmarried People and Widows Should Do."

In this section (17.25-40) Paul takes up a subject about which the Corinthian Christians had written him: should people marry? In the background (see verses 26,29,31) is the belief that the world will soon end and that marriage as a means of propagating the human race is no longer needed. So Paul's concern is that they be effective servants of Christ, giving themselves completely to his service. He does not forbid marriage but he is of the opinion that the unmarried state is preferable. At the end of the section (verses 39-40) Paul teaches what a Christian widow should do.

| 7.25 TEV | RSV |
|---|---|
| Now, concerning what you wrote about unmarried people: I do not have a command from the Lord, but I give my opinion as one who by the Lord's mercy is worthy of trust. | Now concerning the unmarried,$y$ I have no command of the Lord, but I give my opinion as one who by the Lord's mercy is trustworthy. |

$y$ Greek *virgins*

concerning what you wrote: see 7.1.

unmarried people: this translates the Greek "virgins" (see RSV footnote), which is used both of men and women. See further on "virgins" in verse 36.

I do not have a command from the Lord: compare 7.10 and 7.12. Here the Lord is Jesus Christ.

my opinion: the word appears again in verse 40. It is related to the word translated permission in verse 6.

one who by the Lord's mercy is worthy of trust: "because the Lord has shown mercy (or, been merciful) to me, I can be trusted," "the Lord has been merciful to me and he has judged me trustworthy (or, faithful; or, dependable)."

the Lord: either Jesus Christ or God; perhaps the latter.

The verse may be restructured: "...I do not have a command from the Lord, and so I give you my opinion on the subject. The Lord has been merciful to me and so you can trust me."

| 7.26 TEV | RSV |
|---|---|
| Considering the present distress, I think it is better for a man to stay as he is. | I think that in view of the present$m$ distress it is well for a person to remain as he is. |

$m$ Or *impending*

Considering: "Because of," "In light of," "On account of."

the present distress: the word present translates the perfect participle of a Greek verb which means either "to be near" or "to be present." The TEV translation makes it appear that Paul is speaking generally of the troubles and difficulties in which Christians were living. But the verbal form may be understood to mean "impending" (see RSV footnote), that is, close by, soon to appear. This would refer specifically to the end of the age (see verses 29,31), which was expected to come soon. This interpretation seems preferable.

to stay as he is: that is, not try to change his marital status.

| 7.27　　　TEV | RSV |
|---|---|
| Do you have a wife? Then don't try to get rid of her. Are you unmarried? Then don't look for a wife. | Are you bound to a wife? Do not seek to be free. Are you free from a wife? Do not seek marriage. |

Do you have a wife?...Are you unmarried?: this translates what is literally "Are you bound to a wife (or, woman)?...Are you free from a wife (or, woman)?"

get rid of her: "send her away," "divorce her," "leave her."

Are you unmarried?: some take the Greek verb "loosed" to mean "has your marriage been dissolved?" This more restricted meaning is possible, but in the context it would seem the more general meaning is intended.

don't look for a wife: "don't try to get married," "stay single."

| 7.28　　　TEV | RSV |
|---|---|
| But if you do marry, you haven't committed a sin; and if an un-married woman marries, she has-n't committed a sin. But I would rather spare you the everyday troubles that married people will have. | But if you marry, you do not sin, and if a girl[z] marries she does not sin. Yet those who marry will have worldly troubles, and I would spare you that.<br><br>[z]Greek *virgin* |

an unmarried woman: "a single woman," "a girl," "a virgin."

the everyday troubles: this translates "affliction in the flesh." The expression refers to the problems and difficulties married people encounter. Paul may have been speaking from personal experience.

The last sentence may be restructured: "But married people have many troubles, and I would like to keep you from having such troubles (or, difficulties)."

| 7.29　　　TEV | RSV |
|---|---|
| What I mean, my brothers, is this: there is not much time left, and from now on married men should live as though they were not mar-ried; | I mean, brethren, the appointed time has grown very short; from now on, let those who have wives live as though they had none, |

What I mean: Paul explains why he gives them the advice not to change their marital status. "I tell you this...because."

my brothers: see 1.10.

there is not much time left: "the end will come soon," "the time we live in will not last much longer."

married men should live as though they were not married: the sur-face meaning would appear to be that Paul is telling married men to abandon their wives and live a celibate life. But as though makes it clear that Paul is saying that married men should not consider their married state as absolute and final, in light of the fact that the end is near, when all such relationships will become meaningless.

7.30  TEV

those who weep, as though they
were not sad; those who laugh, as
though they were not happy; those
who buy, as though they did not
own what they bought;

RSV

and those who mourn as though they
were not mourning, and those who
rejoice as though they were not
rejoicing, and those who buy as
though they had no goods,

Paul gives the same kind of advice to those who weep, those who
laugh, and those who buy: all such conditions will soon come to an end.
In translation it may be preferable to have complete sentences: "Those
who weep should act as though they were not sad. Those who laugh should
act as though they were not happy. Those who buy things should act as
though those things did not really belong to them."

7.31  TEV

those who deal in material goods,
as though they were not fully occupied with them. For this world,
as it is now, will not last much
longer.

RSV

and those who deal with the world
as though they had no dealings
with it. For the form of this
world is passing away.

those who deal in material goods: "those who are involved in worldly
matters." The phrase material goods translates the Greek word "world."
The translation may be: "Those who use material goods (or, wealth)
should act as though they did not have to use them."
this world, as it is now: "this world in its present form." The
Greek word translated "form" (RSV) means the outward appearance.
will not last much longer: "will soon disappear," "will soon come
to an end."

7.32  TEV

I would like you to be free
from worry. An unmarried man concerns himself with the Lord's work,
because he is trying to please the
Lord.

RSV

I want you to be free from
anxieties. The unmarried man is
anxious about the affairs of the
Lord, how to please the Lord;

to be free from worry: "not to have any anxieties (or, worries)."
concerns himself: the Greek verb is related to the adjective translated free from worry.
the Lord's work: "the work he does for the Lord (Jesus Christ)."
because he is trying to please the Lord: this translates an indirect question in Greek, "how he can please the Lord." The sentence may
be restructured: "An unmarried man is concerned about the work he does
for the Lord; he does all he can to please him."

7.33  TEV

But a married man concerns himself
with worldly matters, because he
wants to please his wife;

RSV

but the married man is anxious
about worldly affairs, how to
please his wife,

The form of this verse in Greek is the same as that of verse 32:
"A married man is concerned with worldly matters (or, everyday matters);
he does all he can to please his wife."

| 7.34 TEV | RSV |
|---|---|
| and so he is pulled in two directions. An unmarried woman or a virgin concerns herself with the Lord's work, because she wants to be dedicated both in body and spirit; but a married woman concerns herself with worldly matters, because she wants to please her husband. | and his interests are divided. And the unmarried woman or girl[z] is anxious about the affairs of the Lord, how to be holy in body and spirit; but the married woman is anxious about worldly affairs, how to please her husband.<br><br>[z]Greek *virgin* |

he is pulled in two directions: "he is divided (in his interests)."
Paul is speaking about a Christian married man; Paul assumes that that
man is trying to please the Lord as well as trying to please his wife,
and so he is motivated by two conflicting loyalties. "He has conflicting
interests" or "his heart is divided" (where "heart" is spoken of as the
seat of affection or loyalty).
An unmarried woman or a virgin: here unmarried woman must refer
either to a widow or to a woman whose marriage has been dissolved.
a virgin: either a woman who has not yet married or else (see
verse 36) a woman who has taken a vow not to marry.
to be dedicated: this translates "to be holy," that is, wholly committed to the Lord's work, completely involved in it.
but a married woman: the form of the Greek text here is the same as
that of verses 32,33. "A married woman is concerned about the work she
does for her husband; she does all she can to please him."
Textual Note: there is a different text for this verse (see KJV),
which seems to mean, "And there is a difference between a wife and a
virgin. An unmarried woman concerns herself with the Lord's work...."
The vast majority of modern translations follow the text represented by
TEV and RSV.

| 7.35 TEV | RSV |
|---|---|
| I am saying this because I want to help you. I am not trying to put restrictions on you. Instead, I want you to do what is right and proper, and to give yourselves completely to the Lord's service without any reservation. | I say this for your own benefit, not to lay any restraint upon you, but to promote good order and to secure your undivided devotion to the Lord. |

Paul carefully explains why he gives them this advice. He is trying to help them. He doesn't want to restrict them in any way, that is,
lay down rules and regulations that would keep them from having a happy
Christian life.

to do what is right and proper: "to live the way you should."
without any reservation: "with all your heart," "without any dis-
tractions."


Introductory Note to Verses 36-38: As the TEV footnotes show, verses
36-38 may be understood in different ways. The differences arise from
the impossibility of determining for certain the exact meaning of the
Greek word *parthenos* ("virgin") in this context. The word means specifically a woman who has never had sexual intercourse, or more generally
an unmarried woman. The same word appears in verses 25,28,34. In verse
25 it is plural and seems to refer to virgins of both sexes; but it is
possible that only the female sex is meant. In verses 28,34 the word
refers to female virgins. In these last two instances (and possibly also
in the first) the word may be understood not in the usual sense of an
unmarried girl but of a woman who has taken a vow to remain unmarried,
to lead a celibate life. This meaning is especially possible in verse 34,
where *parthenos* is used as an additional classification besides "unmarried woman."

In verses 36-38 the word *parthenos* appears always modified by the
masculine possessive pronoun: "his virgin" (verse 36) and "his own virgin" (verses 37,38).

The difficulty in deciding what the verses mean is also caused by
the Greek verb used twice in verse 38; it may mean "to give in marriage"
and so would have as subject the father or guardian of the girl, or else
it may mean "to marry" and so would have as subject the man the girl is
engaged to.

Further trouble is caused by the uncertainty over who is meant by
the Greek adjective in verse 36 which TEV translates "his passions are
too strong." Does it refer to the girl or to the man?

There are three possibilities for understanding the situation in
Corinth that Paul is addressing: (1) the verses are directed to a man
who has an unmarried daughter (or to the guardian of an unmarried girl);
(2) the verses refer to an engaged couple who are uncertain whether or
not they should marry; (3) the verses refer to an engaged couple who
have taken the vow not to marry, or else who live together without any
sexual relationships, a so-called "spiritual marriage."

TEV takes the third choice. The main difficulty with this choice is
that there is no evidence outside this passage that such a condition
existed among Christians in Corinth (or elsewhere) at that time. RSV
seems to take the second choice.

The TEV footnote takes the first choice (also KJV): but this interpretation has been largely abandoned by modern translations. The strongest
case for this interpretation is the fact that the verb that appears
twice in verse 38 is used nowhere else in the New Testament with the
meaning "to marry"; it always means "give in marriage," appearing together with another verb which means "to marry," as follows "(men) marry
and (women) are given in marriage." But one difficulty with this interpretation is that in verse 36 the plural of the verb "to marry" is used,
"they are to marry"—which cannot apply, of course, to a father (or
guardian) and the girl, but only to an engaged couple.

7.36

In his translation of the New Testament, William Barclay provides three different translations of verses 36-38, each one reflecting a different interpretation of the situation.

<table>
<tr><td>7.36 TEV</td><td>RSV</td></tr>
</table>

| 7.36    TEV | RSV |
|---|---|
| In the case of an engaged couple who have decided not to marry: if the man feels that he is not acting properly toward the girl and if his passions are too strong and he feels that they ought to marry, then they should get married, as he wants to.[h] There is no sin in this. | If any one thinks that he is not behaving properly toward his betrothed,[z] if his passions are strong, and it has to be, let him do as he wishes: let them marry— it is no sin.<br><br>[z]Greek *virgin* |

[h]an engaged couple...as he wants to; *or* a man and his unmarried daughter; if he feels that he is not acting properly toward her, and if she is at the right age to marry, then he should do as he wishes and let her get married.

an engaged couple who have decided not to marry: this follows the third possible interpretation. Here RSV does not thus define the relationship; but verse 37 shows clearly that there has been, at least on the part of the man, an initial decision not to marry.

not acting properly: "acting in a way he shouldn't," "behaving in a wrong manner" (that is, by having decided not to marry her).

his passions are too strong: "he cannot control his (sexual) desires."

he feels that they ought to marry: "and he feels he should marry her."

then they should get married, as he wants to: this translates what is literally "he is to do what he wants...they are to marry." The verb "to marry" in Greek is plural.

There is no sin in this: or "He does not sin" (by getting married).

The alternative translation in the TEV footnote will be considered after verse 38.

| 7.37    TEV | RSV |
|---|---|
| But if a man, without being forced to do so, has firmly made up his mind not to marry,[i] and if he has his will under complete control and has already decided in his own mind what to do—then he does well not to marry the girl.[j] | But whoever is firmly established in his heart, being under no necessity but having his desire under control, and has determined this in his heart, to keep her as his betrothed,[z] he will do well. |

$i$not to marry; *or* not to let his      $z$Greek *virgin*
daughter get married.

$j$marry the girl; *or* let her get
married.

     This verse is quite wordy, as Paul elaborately describes the condi-
tions under which a man will decide not to marry.
     <u>without being forced to do so</u>: "and nobody is making him do it,"
"he has freely made the decision himself."
     <u>has firmly made up his mind</u>: "has firmly purposed in his heart,"
"has made a firm decision on the matter."
     <u>then he does well not to marry the girl</u>: this translates what is
literally "(decided) to keep his own virgin (a virgin), he will do well."
     The verse is a long and involved sentence. It may be restructured
as follows: "But it may be that the man, by his own free will, has
firmly made up his mind not to marry. He is completely in control of his
will, and his decision not to marry the girl is final. This man does
well not to get married."

7.38        TEV                             RSV
So the man who marries$k$ does well,    So that he who marries his be-
but the one who doesn't marry$l$ does    trothed$z$ does well; and he who
even better.                              refrains from marriage will do
                                        better.
$k$marries; *or* lets his daughter get
married.                               $z$Greek *virgin*

$l$doesn't marry; *or* doesn't let her
get married.

     Again Paul says it is better not to marry than to marry (as in
verses 7,8-9,28). But he does not condemn marriage as wrong.
     <u>who marries</u>: "who marries his girl."
     If the alternative interpretation represented in the TEV footnotes
is preferred, that is, that the subject of verses 36-38 is a man (or
guardian) and his unmarried daughter (or ward), the translation may be
rendered as follows:

> 36 A man may have made up his mind to keep his
> (virgin) daughter from marrying. But as she
> gets older he may feel that he is not treating
> her properly, and so he decides that she should
> marry. He ought to do as he wishes and let her
> (and her fiancé) get married. There is no sin
> in this. 37 But it may be that he, by his own
> free will, has firmly made up his mind that she
> is not to marry. He is completely in control of
> his will, and his decision that his daughter
> should not marry is final. This man does well
> not to let her marry. 38 So the man who lets

his daughter get married does well, but the man
who doesn't let his daughter get married does
even better.

| 7.39 | TEV | RSV |
|---|---|---|

| | |
|---|---|
| A married woman is not free as long as her husband lives; but if her husband dies, then she is free to be married to any man she wishes, but only if he is a Christian. | A wife is bound to her husband as long as he lives. If the husband dies, she is free to be married to whom she wishes, only in the Lord. |

is not free: "is not free to marry," "is not allowed to marry."
Presumably this includes the case of a woman who is already separated
from her (living) husband. But the surface meaning is that a Christian
woman is not free to divorce her husband and marry another man.
only if he is a Christian: this translates "only in the Lord."
Paul requires that a Christian widow marry only a Christian man.

| 7.40 | TEV | RSV |
|---|---|---|

| | |
|---|---|
| She will be happier, however, if she stays as she is. That is my opinion, and I think that I too have God's Spirit. | But in my judgment she is happier if she remains as she is. And I think that I have the Spirit of God. |

she stays as she is: that is, single.
have God's Spirit: "am controlled (or, led) by the Spirit of God."

# Chapter 8

The Question about Food Offered to Idols

Paul now takes up another question the Corinthian Christians had written him about. Should Christians eat meat that had been offered to idols? The situation that prompted this question was as follows: Only a small part of the slain animal offered as a sacrifice in pagan temples was actually burned on the altar. In many cases, the greater part of the animal, after being ritually offered to the god, was kept by the worshiper, who might then prepare a meal in or near the temple itself, to which he would invite relatives and friends. Could a Christian in good conscience accept such an invitation and eat that meat? Or the worshiper might take the meat home and invite his relatives and friends to a meal at his home. In addition, much of the meat offered in sacrifice would be sold by the priests to markets, where it would be sold to the public. Could a Christian purchase and eat this meat? Some Christians in Corinth believed that they would be guilty of idolatry if they ate such meat. Other Christians, in the confidence that the Christian faith had freed them from any such superstitious fears, tended to look down on their fellow Christians as inferior and weaker in the faith. So Paul deals not only with the question of the meat itself but also with the relation between Christians who differed on the subject.

| 8.1 TEV | RSV |
|---|---|
| Now, concerning what you wrote about food offered to idols. | Now concerning food offered to idols: we know that "all of us possess knowledge." "Knowledge" puffs up, but love builds up. |
| It is true, of course, that "all of us have knowledge," as they say. Such knowledge, however, puffs a person up with pride; but love builds up. | |

Now, concerning what you wrote: see 7.1.

food offered to idols: "meat used in pagan worship," "pieces of meat that had been offered to pagan gods." It is obviously impossible to include in the text all the information needed to allow the reader to understand clearly the background of the question. A cultural footnote here would be helpful.

"all of us have knowledge," as they say: it seems quite evident that "we all have knowledge" was a slogan of some of the Corinthian Christians. They believed that they, as Christians, had superior knowledge which allowed them to act as they pleased.

puffs a person up with pride: "makes a person proud," "fills a person's heart with pride." See the same verb in 4.18.

love builds up: "love makes us grow spiritually," "love makes the Christian fellowship grow." Love here is the Christian's love for his fellow Christians.

| 8.2 TEV | RSV |
|---|---|
| Whoever thinks he knows something really doesn't know as he ought to know. | If any one imagines that he knows something, he does not yet know as he ought to know. |

Paul is pointing out that knowledge that creates pride is not true Christian knowledge. A Christian who thinks himself superior to his fellow Christians because of what he knows does not have the kind of knowledge he should have.

| 8.3 TEV | RSV |
|---|---|
| But the person who loves God is known by him. | But if one loves God, one is known by him. |

This verse does not fit very precisely in the context. One would expect Paul to say something like "But the person who loves has true knowledge," that is, the way to knowledge is through love. But the verb "to know" in Greek is in the passive voice, and the Greek text as we now have it means "The person who loves God is (or, has been) known by him."

| 8.4 TEV | RSV |
|---|---|
| So then, about eating the food offered to idols: we know that an idol stands for something that does not really exist; we know that there is only the one God. | Hence, as to the eating of food offered to idols, we know that "an idol has no real existence," and that "there is no God but one." |

So then, about eating the food offered to idols: "And now to consider (or, answer) the question whether Christians are allowed to eat meat offered to idols (or, meat that was used in pagan sacrifices)." Or, to put the question from the Corinthians in direct form, "And now to answer your question, 'Are Christians allowed to eat meat offered to idols?'"

we know: this is inclusive, "all of us Christians know."

an idol stands for something that does not really exist: this translates "an idol is nothing in the world." Idol worshipers regarded an idol as a representation of a real god, and Paul is denying that such a god actually exists. An idol, in Paul's view, represents something that really does not exist. It may be better to translate "...about eating food (or, meat) that pagans offer to their gods. We know that these gods really do not exist."

there is only one God: "there is no other god besides the real God."

| 8.5 TEV | RSV |
|---|---|
| Even if there are so-called "gods," whether in heaven or on earth, and even though there are many of these "gods" and "lords," | For although there may be so-called gods in heaven or on earth —as indeed there are many "gods" and many "lords"— |

Paul concedes, for the sake of argument, that these gods may actually exist, and that there were many of these gods and heavenly lords in heaven and on earth. The translation could be "Some say that there are gods in heaven and on earth; they believe that there are many gods and many (heavenly) lords."

| 8.6 TEV | RSV |
|---|---|
| yet there is for us only one God, the Father, who is the Creator of all things and for whom we live; and there is only one Lord, Jesus Christ, through whom all things were created and through whom we live. | yet for us there is one God, the Father, from whom are all things and for whom we exist, and one Lord, Jesus Christ, through whom are all things and through whom we exist. |

for us: this is inclusive, "for us Christians." "We Christians believe that there is only one God."

who is the Creator of all things: "by whom all things were created."

for whom we live: or "to whom we are (all) going." God is both the origin and the goal of creation; he created all things and all of us his creatures find our true meaning in him.

through whom all things were created: "by means of whom God created all things." God is the Creator and Christ is the agent of creation. This relationship may be difficult to express. In some languages this is expressed by "God caused Christ to create everything." In others, "God created everything; Christ did it." Or else, using the verb "to help": "God created everything, with Christ helping him." This, however, almost speaks of two creators, not one.

through whom we live: here we is inclusive of all Christians. The role of Christ may be represented by "he gives us life," "he enables us to live," or "we live because of what he has done."

| 8.7 TEV | RSV |
|---|---|
| But not everyone knows this truth. Some people have been so used to idols that to this day when they eat such food they still think of it as food that belongs to an idol; their conscience is weak, and they feel they are defiled by the food. | However, not all possess this knowledge. But some, through being hitherto accustomed to idols, eat food as really offered to an idol; and their conscience, being weak, is defiled. |

But not everyone knows this truth: Paul is talking about the Corinthian Christians, as the following statement shows. By this truth Paul means the fact that there are no gods, only the one God, and so meat offered in temples of pagans can be eaten by Christians with a free conscience.

have been so used to idols: "are so accustomed to the practice of idolatry," "are so familiar with pagan worship." These people, although now Christians, are still ruled by the attitudes they had when they were pagans.

food that belongs to an idol: "meat that has been offered to a pagan God."

their conscience is weak: this concept may be difficult to represent in some languages. The conscience is the center of moral judgments, and it acts, as it were, independently of the choice or decision of a person. A person may know that something is not wrong, yet that person's conscience will still judge the action as wrong and make that person feel guilty. A "weak conscience" is one that is not subject to the person's changed attitude, that does not conform itself to enlightened reason, that still reacts according to former ways of thinking. This would be particularly true in the case of people converted from a pagan religion to the Christian faith. Their Christian faith should have taught them that there were no gods besides the one true God, but their conscience would still react as though other gods existed. And as regarding pagan sacrifices, they would still be unable to shake off the belief that the pagan gods actually ate the sacrifices offered to them.

defiled: that is, made ceremonially or spiritually unfit to worship God. See "unclean" in 7.14 (RSV).

The second sentence of the verse may be translated as follows: "Their Christian faith is still not strong enough, and when they eat meat that has been offered to an idol (or, meat that was used in pagan worship) they feel that they are behaving like pagans."

| 8.8 TEV | RSV |
|---|---|
| Food, however, will not improve our relation with God; we shall not lose anything if we do not eat, nor shall we gain anything if we do eat. | Food will not commend us to God. We are no worse off if we do not eat, and no better off if we do. |

Food: or "Eating food."

will not improve our relation with God: "food will not (or, does not) bring us nearer to God" or "...make us any better in God's sight."

we shall not lose anything: "we are no worse off," "our relation with God is not harmed."

nor shall we gain anything: "nor is our relation with God improved (or, made stronger)."

The verse may be restated, as follows: "Eating some food or the other does not bring us nearer to God. If we eat something, this does not improve our relation with him, and if we don't eat something, this does not weaken our relation with him." Or, "God does not consider us better if we eat something, nor does he consider us worse if we don't eat something."

| 8.9 TEV | RSV |
|---|---|
| Be careful, however, not to let your freedom of action make those who are weak in the faith fall into sin. | Only take care lest this liberty of yours somehow become a stumbling block to the weak. |

your freedom of action: Paul is here speaking to those Corinthian Christians who knew that there was nothing wrong in eating meat sacrificed to idols. What effect would their action have on Christian people who did not believe as they did? Paul says that these people are weak in the faith, that is, their Christian faith is not strong enough to convince them that the eating of meat offered to an idol has no spiritual significance. Paul says that these people will fall into sin. This translates the Greek word "stumbling, fall." The sin is explained in detail in verses 10-13. If possible, the translation should leave the explanation of the sin for verses 10-13, but if some explanation is required in this verse, a translation may say "But you must make sure that your freedom of action (or, freedom to eat meat sacrificed to an idol) will not harm your fellow Christians who are weak in the faith. When they see what you do, they might do the same; but since they think it is wrong, they will be sinning."

| 8.10 TEV | RSV |
|---|---|
| Suppose a person whose conscience is weak in this matter sees you, who have so-called "knowledge," eating in the temple of an idol; will not this encourage him to eat food offered to idols? | For if any one sees you, a man of knowledge, at table in an idol's temple, might he not be encouraged, if his conscience is weak, to eat food offered to idols? |

Paul makes clear what he means in verse 9. He speaks directly to the Christian whose faith and conscience are strong.

whose conscience is weak in this matter: see verse 7.

you, who have so-called "knowledge,": or "you, who have knowledge." TEV says so-called "knowledge" since it is clear that Paul is using "knowledge" here in the sense in which it is used in verses 1-2. This was the proud claim of people for whom "knowledge" was what mattered most, a point of view which Paul criticizes.

eating in the temple of an idol: it was often the custom for worshipers, after offering part of the animal on a pagan altar, to eat the rest of the animal there in the temple. This would be a social occasion and friends would be invited to share in the meal. Among these friends there might be a "strong" Christian, who knew that there was nothing wrong in eating this meat in a pagan temple.

will not this encourage him...idols?: or, as a statement, "He will be encouraged to eat food offered to idols." And in so doing, this person would be doing something that he or she considered sinful.

| 8.11 TEV | RSV |
|---|---|
| And so this weak person, your brother for whom Christ died, will perish because of your "knowledge"! | And so by your knowledge this weak man is destroyed, the brother for whom Christ died. |

weak person: "person whose Christian faith is not strong."

will perish: spiritually; "will be lost."

| 8.12 TEV | RSV |
|---|---|
| And in this way you will be sinning against Christ by sinning against your Christian brothers and wounding their weak conscience. | Thus, sinning against your brethren and wounding their conscience when it is weak, you sin against Christ. |

Paul here explains the consequence of the "strong" Christian's action: he not only sins against his "weak" Christian brother, but sins also against Christ. Christ is identified with the weak brother, and a strong Christian has special responsibilities for the spiritual welfare of his weak brother.

wounding their weak conscience: "making their weak conscience suffer."

The verse may be restructured: "You sin against your Christian brothers and you damage (or, wound) their weak conscience. By doing this you are sinning against Christ."

| 8.13 TEV | RSV |
|---|---|
| So then, if food makes my brother sin, I will never eat meat again, so as not to make my brother fall into sin. | Therefore, if food is a cause of my brother's falling, I will never eat meat, lest I cause my brother to fall. |

if food makes my brother sin: "if my Christian brother believes he is sinning when he eats meat offered to idols."

I will never eat meat again: "I will never again eat meat that has been offered to idols."

so as not to make my brother fall into sin: "because I don't want to make my (weak) brother commit sin," "because I don't want to be responsible for making my brother sin."

# Chapter 9

Rights and Duties of an Apostle: "Paul Defends His Rights as an Apostle."

In this section (9.1-27) Paul writes at length about his rights as an apostle. Evidently there had been considerable criticism of Paul, and some of his opponents were saying that he was not a real apostle, since he had not been one of the twelve disciples of Jesus. Here Paul is concerned to emphasize his right as an apostle to be supported by the churches. Paul has not availed himself of this right, but instead has worked to support himself (verses 1-18). He then discusses briefly his strategy to win all kinds of people to the Christian faith (verses 19-22), and finally speaks of the strict discipline he submits to in order to keep fit spiritually (verses 23-27).

| 9.1 TEV | RSV |
|---|---|
| Am I not a free man? Am I not an apostle? Haven't I seen Jesus our Lord? And aren't you the result of my work for the Lord? | Am I not free? Am I not an apostle? Have I not seen Jesus our Lord? Are not you my workmanship in the Lord? |

Paul begins his defense with four strong rhetorical questions. Writing with considerable heat, he immediately challenges his critics by stating what is self-evident. They can only answer "Yes" to all four of his questions and thus will have to admit that he is indeed a genuine apostle.

In some languages it may be preferable to recast the questions as strong statements of fact: "I am, indeed, a free man" or "You must admit that I am a free man, that I am an apostle..." and so forth.

a free man: the "freedom" of which Paul speaks here is the spiritual freedom from sin, superstition, and legalism (see also verse 19). The reverse statement may be preferable: "I am not a slave to sin and legalism" or "I am free from the bondage of sin and legalism."

apostle: see 1.1.

Haven't I seen Jesus our Lord?: as a statement, this could be said, "You know that our Lord Jesus appeared to me."

seen: Paul here refers to the appearance of the risen Lord to him (see 15.8). It is not to be inferred from this text that Paul had actually seen Jesus during Jesus' lifetime in Palestine. Jesus our Lord is the title given to Jesus as the resurrected Lord of God's people; our here is all-inclusive.

aren't you the result of my work for the Lord?: Paul is here speaking of the fact that he had preached in Corinth and that the Corinthian Christians had come to accept Christ as Lord as a result of his ministry among them. "You are believers (or, Christians) as the result of my work (or, because I proclaimed the Good News to you)."

Textual Note: in some inferior manuscripts (see KJV) the first two questions are reversed; and some manuscripts have "Jesus Christ our Lord" instead of the better text "Jesus our Lord."

| 9.2 TEV | RSV |
|---|---|
| Even if others do not accept me as an apostle, surely you do! Because of your life in union with the Lord you yourselves are proof of the fact that I am an apostle. | If to others I am not an apostle, at least I am to you; for you are the seal of my apostleship in the Lord. |

do not accept me as an apostle: "think (or, say) that I am not an apostle." Or the whole statement may be reversed: "Surely you accept me as an apostle (or, admit that I am an apostle) even though other people do not."

Because of your life in union with the Lord: "Because you are Christians (or, believers)." "The fact that you are Christians (or, believers) is proof of the fact that I am an apostle."

in union with the Lord: see 1.2.

proof of the fact that I am an apostle: this translates "the seal of my apostleship." The word "seal" is used here in a figurative sense of "confirmation," "guarantee," "proof of genuineness (or, authenticity)." The "seal" was the Lord's own signature, so to speak, on the document stating that Paul was an apostle.

| 9.3 TEV | RSV |
|---|---|
| When people criticize me, this is how I defend myself: | This is my defense to those who would examine me. |

criticize me: "judge me," "condemn me"—that is, express doubts that Paul is an apostle. "This is how I defend myself against those who judge (or, condemn) me," or "...against those who say I am not an apostle."

| 9.4 TEV | RSV |
|---|---|
| Don't I have the right to be given food and drink for my work? | Do we not have the right to our food and drink? |

Here the Greek text has the plural "Don't we have the right." It may be that Paul is speaking generally of all apostles, or else of Barnabas and himself. But it is possible that he is speaking only of himself as a representative of all apostles, and many translations use the first person singular, I. One of the rights of an apostle was to be supported by the churches and to not have to work for a living.

A statement may be preferable to the rhetorical question: "I (or, We apostles) have the right to be given (or, to receive) food and drink for my (or, our) work as an apostle."

food and drink: this stands for material support in general and not just food and drink as such.

| 9.5 TEV | RSV |
|---|---|
| Don't I have the right to follow the example of the other apostles | Do we not have the right to be accompanied by a wife,[n] as the |

and the Lord's brothers and Peter, by taking a Christian wife with me on my trips?

other apostles and the brothers of the Lord and Cephas?

[n]Greek *a sister as wife*

Here Paul claims the right to take a Christian wife with him on his travels—in which case she, too, should be supported by the Christian communities. It is to be noted (verses 12b,15) that Paul explicitly says he has not made use of any of these rights. But in order for this to apply to Paul personally he would have had to have a Christian wife, and what Paul has already said in 8.7-8 makes clear that he did not have a wife. So his claim is that if he in fact did have a Christian wife, he had the right, as an apostle, to take her with him on his missionary travels.

the other apostles: this refers not only to the Twelve, but to all others who were apostles (see 15.5,7).

the Lord's brothers: elsewhere (see 15.7; Gal 1.19) Paul refers only to one brother, James; Mark 6.3 gives the names of the brothers of Jesus. The reference here implies that they are all believers.

Peter: referred to already in 1.12; for his marital status, see Mark 1.30.

This verse may be translated as a statement: "I also have the right to take a Christian wife with me on my travels, just as the other apostles and the Lord's brothers and Peter do." Or the order can be changed: "The other apostles and the Lord's brothers and Peter take their wives with them on their travels. So I also have the right to take a Christian wife with me on my travels."

9.6          TEV
Or are Barnabas and I the only ones who have to work for our living?

RSV
Or is it only Barnabas and I who have no right to refrain from working for a living?

Barnabas: mentioned only here in this letter. In his early ministry Paul had Barnabas as a companion (see Acts 13.1—15.23).

The verse may be translated in the form of a statement: "Barnabas and I are not the only apostles who have to work for our living (or, work to support ourselves)."

9.7          TEV
What soldier ever has to pay his own expenses in the army? What farmer does not eat the grapes from his own vineyard? What shepherd does not use the milk from his own sheep?

RSV
Who serves as a soldier at his own expense? Who plants a vineyard without eating any of its fruit? Who tends a flock without getting some of the milk?

Paul uses three examples to show that apostles have the right to be paid for their work. As a statement, the first example may be translated, "No man has to pay his own expenses while he is serving in the army," or

"No soldier has to pay his own expenses."

farmer: this translates "someone who plants a vineyard." "A man who plants a vineyard has the right to eat the grapes." If vineyard and grapes are unknown, a cultural substitute may be used, either in terms of cereals or of fruit trees that are cultivated.

shepherd: this translates "someone who tends a flock." "A man who takes care of sheep has the right to use the milk the sheep give."

All three examples are cited to show that in any profession there are certain rights and privileges which no one denies.

| 9.8 TEV | RSV |
|---|---|
| I don't have to limit myself to these everyday examples, because the Law says the same thing. | Do I say this on human authority? Does not the law say the same? |

I don't have to limit myself to these everyday examples: or, following another interpretation, "This is not just my own opinion" or "I don't have to rely on human reasoning alone." Probably the latter is more in keeping with the context, since what follows is an explicit statement from the Scriptures.

the Law says: or "the Scriptures say."

| 9.9 TEV | RSV |
|---|---|
| We read in the Law of Moses, "Do not muzzle an ox when you are using it to thresh grain." Now, is God concerned about oxen? | For it is written in the law of Moses, "You shall not muzzle an ox when it is treading out the grain." Is it for oxen that God is concerned? |

Paul quotes Deuteronomy 25.4. Threshing is the process by which the grains of wheat are separated from the straw. The stalks of wheat (or, barley) were laid flat on the ground, and an ox would be driven around over the stalks, trampling them with his feet. The Law prohibited tying the animal's mouth in order to keep it from eating any of the stalks.

Now, is God concerned about oxen?: or "God is not really concerned about oxen." Paul here disregards the primary meaning of the text in order to apply it to Christian apostles.

| 9.10 TEV | RSV |
|---|---|
| Didn't he really mean us when he said that? Of course that was written for us. The man who plows and the man who reaps should do their work in the hope of getting a share of the crop. | Does he not speak entirely for our sake? It was written for our sake, because the plowman should plow in hope and the thresher thresh in hope of a share in the crop. |

Here Paul answers his own question, so the question form should be retained in translation. "Didn't God have us in mind when he said that? Of course that command was written about us apostles."

The man who plows and the man who reaps: Paul uses these examples from everyday life in order to apply them to the work of the apostles. If the singular form should be misleading, plural forms may be used: "Men who plow and men who reap." For the second function, the Greek has "the man who threshes (the grain)." This was done by beating the stalks with a stick to separate the heads of grain.

a share of the crop: or "a share of the grain."


| 9.11       TEV | RSV |
|---|---|
| We have sown spiritual seed among you. Is it too much if we reap material benefits from you? | If we have sown spiritual good among you, is it too much if we reap your material benefits? |

We have sown...we reap: again it is difficult to decide whether Paul is talking about apostles in general or if he is speaking about himself. Since in verse 15 the Greek text switches to the singular, perhaps it is better to keep the plural in verses 11-14.

spiritual seed: Paul is talking about preaching the Gospel. If the figure is hard to understand, the following may be said: "When we preached the gospel to you we were, so to speak, sowing spiritual seed among you," or "We sowed the kind of seed that produced a harvest of spiritual blessings for you."

Is it too much...?: "Is it unreasonable," "Are we expecting too much." Or else, as a statement, "That is why it is not too much...."

material benefits: Paul is speaking quite explicitly of being provided the necessities of life so that the apostles will not have to work to support themselves.


| 9.12       TEV | RSV |
|---|---|
| If others have the right to expect this from you, don't we have an even greater right? | If others share this rightful claim upon you, do not we still more? |
| But we haven't made use of this right. Instead, we have endured everything in order not to put any obstacle in the way of the Good News about Christ. | Nevertheless, we have not made use of this right, but we endure anything rather than put an obstacle in the way of the gospel of Christ. |

If others have the right...?: this long question can be turned into two (or more) statements: "Others are demanding this of you. And we have an even greater right to do so, but we haven't done so."

others: "other apostles," "other Christian workers."

to expect this from you: "to these benefits."

But we haven't made use of this right: it is difficult to decide who is included in this we. Paul is certainly speaking about himself; is he also including Barnabas? Or perhaps Sosthenes (1.1)? It seems that nearly all other apostles made use of their rights, so the singular "I haven't made use of this right" seems more natural—and so some translations have the singular. (But in verse 15 the Greek text switches to the singular.)

we have endured: or "we endure," "we put up with."

everything: "all kinds of troubles (or, difficulties)."

not to put any obstacle: this involves a double negative (obstacle has the idea of "not allowing"), so it may be preferable to express the idea in affirmative terms. "We put up with all kinds of trouble in order to allow the Good News about Christ to go (or, spread) everywhere as quickly as possible."

9.13          TEV                                    RSV

| Surely you know that the men who | Do you not know that those who are |
| work in the Temple get their food | employed in the temple service get |
| from the Temple and that those who | their food from the temple, and |
| offer the sacrifices on the altar | those who serve at the altar share |
| get a share of the sacrifices. | in the sacrificial offerings? |

Paul here refers to the Temple in Jerusalem and the Jewish sacrificial system. The priests and Levites who served in the Temple were given a share of the grain and of the animals offered in sacrifice by the people—that is, they did not have to pay for their own food (see Num 18.8—9.31; Deut 18.1-4).

get their food from the Temple: "eat the food that is used for the sacred offerings," or else, "made their living from working in the Temple."

who offer the sacrifices...get a share of the sacrifices: "who offer the animals in sacrifice on the altar get a share of the meat."

9.14          TEV                                    RSV

| In the same way, the Lord has or- | In the same way, the Lord commanded |
| dered that those who preach the | that those who proclaim the gospel |
| gospel should get their living | should get their living by the |
| from it. | gospel. |

the Lord: here Paul refers to Christ and to what he said, as recorded in Matthew 10.10; Luke 10.7. It might be useful to include the inclusive "us" as the object of the verb: "the Lord has ordered (or, commanded) us...."

get their living from it: "should be paid for doing it," "should have their needs taken care of for the work they do."

9.15          TEV                                    RSV

| But I haven't made use of any | But I have made no use of any |
| of these rights, nor am I writing | of these rights, nor am I writing |
| this now in order to claim such | this to secure any such provision. |
| rights for myself. I would rather | For I would rather die than have |
| die first! Nobody is going to turn | any one deprive me of my ground |
| my rightful boast into empty words! | for boasting. |

Here Paul reaffirms in the first person singular what he said in verse 12b in the plural. Paul states that he has not accepted help from the churches but has worked to support himself.

to claim such rights: "to ask for these benefits."

I would rather die first!: TEV has joined this to what precedes, that is, Paul would rather die than to ask the Corinthians to pay for his work as an apostle. But other translations join it to what follows: "I would rather die than let anyone turn my boast into empty words."

Nobody is going to turn my rightful boast into empty words!: "I will not allow anyone to deprive me of my right to boast."


| 9.16 TEV | RSV |
|---|---|
| I have no right to boast just because I preach the gospel. After all, I am under orders to do so. And how terrible it would be for me if I did not preach the gospel! | For if I preach the gospel, that gives me no ground for boasting. For necessity is laid upon me. Woe to me if I do not preach the gospel! |

After boasting, Paul says that he really has no reason for boasting: "Even though I preach the gospel, I have no reason for boasting." Paul does not say so explicitly, but here he means "Even though I preach the gospel *without being paid for it,*" since this is the topic governing the whole section.

I am under orders to do so: this translates what is literally "necessity (or, compulsion) has been laid upon me." Paul had not volunteered; he had been ordered by the risen Lord to proclaim the gospel.

how terrible it would be: "what a miserable person I would be," "what a tragedy it would be for me." The implied idea is that the Lord would punish him if he did not proclaim the Good News.


| 9.17 TEV | RSV |
|---|---|
| If I did my work as a matter of free choice, then I could expect to be paid; but I do it as a matter of duty, because God has entrusted me with this task. | For if I do this of my own will, I have a reward; but if not of my own will, I am entrusted with a commission. |

Continuing the idea of the compulsion that has been laid upon him to preach the gospel, Paul shows the difference between preaching as a free choice on his part and preaching as a duty.

as a matter of free choice: "because I myself chose (or, decided) to do so."

I could expect to be paid: "I would be earning my wages (or, pay)," "I would have the right to be paid," or "I would expect God to pay (or, reward) me."

as a matter of duty: "because I am forced to do so." The Greek word here is "unwilling," as the opposite of "willing" in the preceding sentence.

because God has entrusted me with this task: "this shows that I have been given a commission." The figure Paul uses is that of a steward, a man who receives his orders directly from the owner of the business or the household. The passive "I have been entrusted" has God as the implied agent.

[ 85 ]

9.18      TEV

What pay do I get, then? It is the
privilege of preaching the Good
News without charging for it, without claiming my rights in my work
for the gospel.

RSV

What then is my reward? Just this:
that in my preaching I may make
the gospel free of charge, not
making full use of my right in the
gospel.

What pay do I get, then?: "What is my reward? or "What do I receive as wages?"
      the privilege: "the right," "the opportunity."
      without claiming my rights: "so as not to claim all my rights."
      in my work for the gospel: or "in the work of preaching the gospel."
The sentence may be translated: "My pay (or, reward) is to be able to
preach the gospel and not charge (or, get paid) for my work. By doing
this I do not claim all the rights I have as a preacher of the Good News."


9.19      TEV

      I am a free man, nobody's
slave; but I make myself everybody's
slave in order to win as many people
as possible.

RSV

      For though I am free from all
men, I have made myself a slave to
all, that I might win the more.

Here Paul leaves off a direct discussion of his rights as an
apostle. It may be appropriate to begin a new section here (9.19-27) with
the heading: "Paul Wants to Win All People to Christ," "Paul's Freedom
as an Apostle."
      I am a free man: as the following discussion shows, Paul's claim is
that he is not governed by the legalism and superstition that govern the
lives of other people; he is free to adapt himself to all conditions
without violating his own principles as a believer.
      nobody's slave: this may be expressed as a full sentence: "No per-
son is my master."
      I make myself everybody's slave: "I act as though everyone else
were my master" or "...as though everyone else had the right to command
me."
      to win: that is, to the gospel, to Jesus Christ.


9.20      TEV

While working with the Jews, I live
like a Jew in order to win them;
and even though I myself am not
subject to the Law of Moses, I live
as though I were when working with
those who are, in order to win them.

RSV

To the Jews I became as a Jew, in
order to win Jews; to those under
the law I became as one under the
law—though not being myself under the law—that I might win
those under the law.

While working with the Jews: "When I preach the gospel to the Jews."
      I live like a Jew: that is, he follows the rules and regulations of
the Law which faithful Jews followed.
      In the second part of the verse Paul repeats, in different words,

what he has already said: "When I preach the gospel to those who obey the Law of Moses, I act (or, live) as though I also were subject to the Law." Then he adds, almost parenthetically, "even though I myself am not subject to the Law." It should be noticed that those who are (subject to the Law of Moses) are the same people, the Jews; in translation it should not appear that Paul was talking about two different groups.

The TEV text is rather complex and it may be necessary to express the meaning in a more simple fashion: "When I preach the gospel to those who are subject to the Law of Moses I live as though I, too, were subject to the Law. (But I really am not subject to the Law.) I do this so as to be able to win to Christ those who are subject to the Law."

| 9.21 TEV | RSV |
|---|---|
| In the same way, when working with Gentiles, I live like a Gentile, outside the Jewish Law, in order to win Gentiles. This does not mean that I don't obey God's law; I am really under Christ's law. | To those outside the law I became as one outside the law—not being without law toward God but under the law of Christ—that I might win those outside the law. |

Gentiles: this translates the Greek "those not under the Law."

I live like a Gentile, outside the Jewish Law: by this Paul means that when he preached the gospel to the Gentiles he, like them, did not observe the ceremonial laws having to do especially with unclean foods.

The whole verse may be restructured as follows: "When working with Gentiles I do not try to obey the Jewish Law. I live as the Gentiles do in order to win them to Christ. I really obey God's law because I live according to Christ's law."

Paul does not equate all Jewish laws with God's law; so he says "This doesn't mean that I disobey God's law; I am subject to Christ's law." In all these instances Paul uses the same word, translated "law." If possible, a translation should use the same word in all these contexts (Jewish Law; God's law; Christ's law): "order, commandment, authority."

| 9.22 TEV | RSV |
|---|---|
| Among the weak in faith I become weak like one of them, in order to win them. So I become all things to all men, that I may save some of them by whatever means are possible. | To the weak I become weak, that I might win the weak. I have become all things to all men, that I might by all means save some. |

weak in faith: here Paul is talking about Christians (see 8.7,9) whose faith is not mature enough and who are still ruled by certain scruples and superstitions. Paul does not despise them; rather he respects their limitations and acts as though he were bound by the same limitations in order to win them also to a full adherence to Christ as Lord.

I become all things to all men: "I adapt myself to the needs (or, conditions) of all kinds of people," "I live (or, act) like all the kinds of people to whom I preach the gospel."

save: here Paul uses another word, but the meaning is the same as "to win" in verses 19-22a. It means to lead people to a saving faith in Christ Jesus as Lord.

by whatever means are possible: "in any way possible," "by any means that are necessary."

| 9.23 | TEV | RSV |
|---|---|---|
| | All this I do for the gospel's sake, in order to share in its blessings. | I do it all for the sake of the gospel, that I may share in its blessings. |

Most translations place this verse with the preceding paragraph and begain a new paragraph in verse 24. It is a transition verse, summarizing what the apostle has just said—and it is probably better to use it to close the preceding paragraph.

for the gospel's sake: "so that the gospel will spread everywhere" or "because of my dedication to the (preaching of the) gospel."

in order to share in its blessings: the Greek says "in order to become its partner," which may be understood to mean "in order to do my share in proclaiming it." Or, following the TEV interpretation, "in order to have a share in what it promises.

| 9.24 | TEV | RSV |
|---|---|---|
| | Surely you know that many runners take part in a race, but only one of them wins the prize. Run, then, in such a way as to win the prize. | Do you not know that in a race all the runners compete, but only one receives the prize? So run that you may obtain it. |

Using the figure of a runner in a race, Paul encourages his readers to be faithful Christians.

many runners take part in a race: this translates "the runners in the stadium all run." Paul is talking about a public sports event in which runners competed for the prize.

Run: here Paul switches from the literal meaning of running a race to the figurative meaning of living the Christian life. If the figurative use of the verb should prove difficult or misleading, a translation could say: "Do your best to live a good Christian life, just as a runner runs the fastest he can; and in this way you will win the prize."

| 9.25 | TEV | RSV |
|---|---|---|
| | Every athlete in training submits to strict discipline, in order to be crowned with a wreath that will not last; but we do it for one that will last forever. | Every athlete exercises self-control in all things. They do it to receive a perishable wreath, but we an imperishable. |

Every athlete in training submits to strict discipline: "Anyone who wants to take part in a race submits himself to (or, undergoes) rigorous training."

a wreath that will not last: a wreath made of laurel leaves was placed on the head of the winner in a race.

    we do it: "we submit to strict discipline," "we undergo rigorous training." Here again Paul switches from the literal to the figurative meaning. A translation may have to make this clear: "We are like those athletes: we Christians submit to strict discipline in order to win a prize that will last forever." It may be necessary to say "prize" instead of "wreath," since "an eternal wreath" may be misleading. So it may help to say in the first part of the verse "in order to win a prize that will not last very long" (instead of in order to be crowned with a wreath that will not last).

| 9.26 TEV | RSV |
|---|---|
| That is why I run straight for the finish line; that is why I am like a boxer who does not waste his punches. | Well, I do not run aimlessly, I do not box as one beating the air; |

    That is why: this relates back to the command in verse 24, "Run, then, in such a way as to win the prize." It may be better to expand this somewhat: "In order to win the prize I run straight..."

    I run straight for the finish line: a runner sets his eyes on the finish line and runs straight for it without veering to the right or to the left. This is a figure of single-minded determination; a Christian has one goal, one aim, and lets nothing distract him from reaching that goal.

    like a boxer: here Paul changes the figure from a runner to a boxer, who tries to make every blow count; he wants to hit his opponent every time he strikes, "like a boxer who tries to make every punch count," "like a boxer who always hits his opponent."

| 9.27 TEV | RSV |
|---|---|
| I harden my body with blows and bring it under complete control, to keep myself from being disqualified after having called others to the contest. | but I pommel my body and subdue it, lest after preaching to others I myself should be disqualified. |

    I harden my body with blows and bring it under complete control: the two Greek verbs mean "to hit a knockout blow" and "to subdue, to lead captive." Paul is not talking about punishment (as it might appear) but about discipline; that is why TEV says harden...with blows, since "to beat" or "to bruise" would give the idea of punishment.

    Paul explains the reason for his rigorous self-discipline by using still another figure: that of a herald who called the competitors to the athletic contest and explained to them the rules they must observe in order to qualify for the prize. Paul sees himself not only as a herald but also as a contestant in the (Christian) race.

    disqualified: that is, unable to take part in the contest because he has not obeyed the rules.

The second part of the verse may be rendered: "If I don't do this, it could happen that after I had called others to take part in the race I myself might not be qualified to run." This, of course, maintains the language of an actual race, and if this should prove difficult to understand, the meaning could be expressed otherwise: "I have proclaimed to others the rules they must obey in order to be faithful Christians. So I have to submit myself to those same rules, that I also may qualify for the prize which is offered to faithful Christians."

# Chapter 10

Warnings against Idols: "Paul Tells His Readers to Avoid Idolatry."
In this section (10.1—11.1) Paul discusses idolatry. First he cites
the experience of the people of Israel in the Old Testament (10.1-10);
from those experiences he draws some general conclusions (10.11-13); then
he addresses the problems the Corinthian Christians are facing (10.14-22)
and concludes with a statement of principles and warnings (10.23—11.1).
Some translations provide a separate section for 10.23—11.1 (see below).

Paul had already discussed the matter of eating food offered to
idols (see 8.1-13), and here he again discusses the problem in the
broader context of faithfulness to God.

| 10.1 TEV | RSV |
|---|---|
| I want you to remember, my brothers, what happened to our ancestors who followed Moses. They were all under the protection of the cloud, and all passed safely through the Red Sea. | I want you to know, brethren, that our fathers were all under the cloud, and all passed through the sea, |

I want you to remember: "You should keep in mind," "You should
never forget." Paul is not informing them of something they did not know;
he is recalling certain matters written in the Old Testament.

my brothers: see 1.10.

our ancestors who followed Moses: the Greek says simply "our ancestors" (literally "our fathers"); TEV has seen fit to make the meaning
clearer by adding who followed Moses; another way would be to say "our
ancestors who were set free from Egypt." The adjective our is inclusive;
and although Paul's readers were not all Jews, in the spiritual sense
the ancient Hebrews are "ancestors" of all Christians, whether Jews or
Gentiles.

under the protection of the cloud: or "guided by the cloud" (see
Exo 13.21-22). The cloud not only guided the Israelites but also pro-
tected them when they crossed the sea (see Exo 14.19-20).

passed safely through the Red Sea: see Exodus 14.22-29. Red Sea translates the Greek "the sea," a reference to the body of water the Hebrews
crossed, which in the Hebrew Old Testament is called "Sea of Reeds." It
is quite certain that it was not what is today called the Red Sea; the
name "Red Sea" comes from the Septuagint, the ancient Greek translation
of the Old Testament, and has been current in English translations. German translations, however, since Luther, have "Sea of Reeds," as do some
modern French translations.

| 10.2 TEV | RSV |
|---|---|
| In the cloud and in the sea they were all baptized as followers of Moses. | and all were baptized into Moses in the cloud and in the sea, |

Paul interprets those historical events as types, that is, they pointed forward to matters having to do with the Christian people.

baptized as followers of Moses: this translates what is in Greek "baptized into Moses." The meaning may be expressed "baptized into union (or, fellowship) with Moses." Some translations say "they were baptized, so to speak," in order to make clear the unusual sense of "baptized" in this verse. Whatever is done, it is important to use the verb "to baptize."

| 10.3-4 TEV | RSV |
|---|---|
| All ate the same spiritual bread 4 and drank the same spiritual drink. They drank from the spiritual rock that went with them; and that rock was Christ himself. | and all ate the same supernatural$^O$ food 4 and all drank the same supernatural$^O$ drink. For they drank from the supernatural$^O$ Rock which followed them, and the Rock was Christ. |

$^O$Greek *spiritual*

spiritual bread: this refers to the manna (see Exo 16.31-35). Instead of bread a translation may say "food." The adjective spiritual may better be translated as "supernatural" (so many translations), since the manna was actually food and the water was really water. Or else, "they ate the special food and drank the special drink (or, water) that God supplied."

As the cloud and the crossing of the sea represent here for Paul a type, or symbol, of Christian baptism, so the bread and the drink stand for the bread and wine of the Lord's Supper.

spiritual drink: this refers to two incidents in the Old Testament: the water from the rock at Rephidim (Exo 17.6) and at Kadesh (Num 20.11).

the spiritual rock that went with them: Paul here seems to refer to a Jewish popular tradition, according to which the rock from which the Hebrews drank water on the two separate occasions was the same rock, and it followed them during their wanderings in the wilderness. Paul identifies this rock with Christ himself. "They drank water from the supernatural rock (or, the rock that God provided) which went with them. That rock was Christ himself."

| 10.5 TEV | RSV |
|---|---|
| But even then God was not pleased with most of them, and so their dead bodies were scattered over the desert. | Nevertheless with most of them God was not pleased; for they were overthrown in the wilderness. |

But even then: this is a strong adversative. "But, in spite of all that God did," "But, even though God had done all this for them."

their dead bodies were scattered over the desert: "they died and their bodies (or, corpses) were scattered over the desert"; or "they died in the desert."

10.6      TEV

    Now, all of this is an example for us, to warn us not to desire evil things, as they did,

RSV

    Now these things are warnings for us, not to desire evil as they did.

    an example for us, to warn us: here us means Christians in general; example...to warn us: or "as symbols to warn us," "symbolic warnings."
    desire evil things: Paul does not specify what these things are for his readers, nor what they were for the Hebrews; "desire things that are wrong (or, sinful)," "to be filled with evil desires."

10.7      TEV

nor to worship idols, as some of them did. As the scripture says, "The people sat down to a feast which turned into an orgy of drinking and sex."

RSV

Do not be idolaters as some of them were; as it is written, "The people sat down to eat and drink and rose up to dance."

    worship idols: "worship false gods," "worship beings that are not God." Paul quotes Exodus 32.6.
    which turned into an orgy of drinking and sex: literally "and they rose to play (or, to dance)." The scene described in Exodus 32.1-19 shows that the worship of the gold bull involved the kind of orgy associated with fertility rites (the bull was a god of fertility), including both excessive drinking and unlawful sexual activity. More general language may be used: "The people sat down to a feast and then had a heathen celebration." The verb "play" should not be used in the sense of innocent frivolity.

10.8      TEV

We must not be guilty of sexual immorality, as some of them were—and in one day twenty-three thousand of them fell dead.

RSV

We must not indulge in immorality as some of them did, and twenty-three thousand fell in a single day.

    sexual immorality: "fornication," "illicit sexual intercourse." This verse refers to the incident at Peor, where the people of Israel were guilty of idolatry and immorality (Num 25.1-9). The Old Testament account gives twenty-four thousand as the number of people who died.
    fell dead: or "were killed." Or, to be more explicit, "and in one day God killed twenty-three thousand of them."

10.9      TEV

We must not put the Lord[m] to the test, as some of them did—and they were killed by snakes.

RSV

We must not put the Lord[p] to the test, as some of them did and were destroyed by serpents;

[m]the Lord; *some manuscripts have* Christ.

[p]Other ancient authorities read *Christ*

put the Lord to the test: "try the Lord's patience," "defy the Lord's order." The incident here referred to is found in Numbers 21.5-6.

As the TEV footnote shows, some Greek manuscripts have "Christ" (or, "the Messiah"). The United Bible Societies' Greek New Testament prefers "Christ" as the word that more likely was in the original text, and so "put Christ to the test" would be the better translation.

| 10.10 TEV | RSV |
|---|---|
| We must not complain, as some of them did—and they were destroyed by the Angel of Death. | nor grumble, as some of them did and were destroyed by the Destroyer. |

complain: "grumble." Paul is here referring to Numbers 16.41-49. The Greek text has the second person plural, "You must not grumble"; TEV has kept the first person plural, in line with the verbs in verses 8,9.

the Angel of Death: literally "the Destroyer." The Old Testament text speaks of a plague, or epidemic, which killed the people. The expression "the Destroyer" is used in Exodus 12.23, referring to the death of the first-born sons in Egypt (and see also Heb 11.28).

| 10.11 TEV | RSV |
|---|---|
| All these things happened to them as examples for others, and they were written down as a warning for us. For we live at a time when the end is about to come. | Now these things happened to them as a warning, but they were written down for our instruction, upon whom the end of the ages has come. |

Paul here repeats the statement he has made in verse 6; examples for others: "to show others what would (or, could) happen." Or the Greek may be understood to mean "as examples for us" (as in verse 6).

they were written down: this refers specifically to the Old Testament record of these events; "people wrote them down," "they are recorded in the Scriptures."

us is here inclusive of all Christians.

For we live in a time when the end is about to come: or "...when the world is about to come to an end." Paul has already alluded to this belief in 7.26,29,31.

the end: "the end of the world (or, the age in which we live)."

is about to come: "will soon arrive." Paul's argument is that since there isn't much time left, the warnings from the history of the people of Israel are especially important for Christians.

| 10.12 TEV | RSV |
|---|---|
| Whoever thinks he is standing firm had better be careful that he does not fall. | Therefore let any one who thinks that he stands take heed lest he fall. |

standing firm...fall: these are figures of spiritual stability, of spiritual safety. It is a warning against self-satisfaction and complacency. "Whoever thinks his faith is strong" or "Whoever thinks that he is in a good condition, in God's sight."

| 10.13 TEV | RSV |
|---|---|
| Every test that you have experienced is the kind that normally comes to people. But God keeps his promise, and he will not allow you to be tested beyond your power to remain firm; at the time you are put to the test, he will give you the strength to endure it, and so provide you with a way out. | No temptation has overtaken you that is not common to man. God is faithful, and he will not let you be tempted beyond your strength, but with the temptation will also provide the way of escape, that you may be able to endure it. |

test: or "temptation." This refers to any kind of difficulty or trouble that makes the Corinthian Christians wonder if their faith in God is justified, or which may make them lose their faith.

is the kind that normally comes to people: "is the kind that everyone experiences," "is the ordinary kind of test (or, temptation)."

beyond your power to remain firm: "beyond your power to bear it"; or "God will not allow a test (or, temptation) to come which you are not (spiritually) strong enough to endure."

The latter part of the verse is usually translated as RSV has done, that is, God makes it possible for a believer to endure the test (or, temptation) by providing a way to escape it. This, however, seems to involve a logical inconsistency, unless it means that a believer, knowing that God will bring the test to an end, is able to endure it.

TEV, however, takes the final genitive phrase "to be able to endure" as a genitive of definition and not of result, which means that "the way out" is the ability to endure the test. So NEB "but when the test comes he will at the same time provide a way out, by enabling you to sustain it."

| 10.14 TEV | RSV |
|---|---|
| So then, my dear friends, keep away from the worship of idols. | Therefore, my beloved, shun the worship of idols. |

Paul here takes up the specific matter of eating meat sacrificed to idols and partaking of the Lord's Supper. Some translations have a new section here (10.14-22), which may have as a heading "Warning against Idolatry" (in which case the section 10.1-13 may be entitled, "Lessons from the History of Israel").

Paul's argument here is as follows: at the Lord's Supper, believers have fellowship with the Lord Jesus (verses 14-17); the Israelites, in their sacrifices, have fellowship with God (verse 18); so in the same way eating meat offered to idols means fellowship with idols (verses 19-22). But Paul does not hold that the analogy is exact, since pagan gods have no real existence.

keep away from: "avoid," "shun," "have nothing to do with," "flee."

| 10.15 TEV | RSV |
|---|---|
| I speak to you as sensible people; judge for yourselves what I say. | I speak as to sensible men; judge for yourselves what I say. |

    sensible: "wise," "intelligent"; "people who have understanding."

| 10.16 TEV | RSV |
|---|---|
| The cup we use in the Lord's Supper and for which we give thanks to God: when we drink from it, we are sharing in the blood of Christ. And the bread we break: when we eat it, we are sharing in the body of Christ. | The cup of blessing which we bless, is it not a participation[q] in the blood of Christ? The bread which we break, is it not a participation[q] in the body of Christ? |

*q*Or *communion*

    This verse is composed of two rhetorical questions (see RSV) which TEV has represented as statements of fact. The literal "The cup of blessing which we bless" (RSV) refers to the cup of wine used in celebrating the Lord's Supper. The noun translated "blessing" and the verb translated "bless" should be understood as "thanksgiving" and "give thanks." If the sense of "to bless" is expressed, it means "to ask God to bless," since by definition a person does not "bless" another person or an object. It seems better to take the verb and noun here in the sense of "give thanks" (see TEV translation of Mark 14.22, where the same Greek verb is used).
    when we drink from it, we are sharing: this translates the Greek "is not the cup...fellowship...?" Of course it is not the cup itself, as a material object, which constitutes the sharing or fellowship; it is the use of it in the Lord's Supper, so TEV has made this explicit.
    sharing in the blood of Christ: given the importance of "the blood" and "the body" in the celebration of the Lord's Supper, it is better to use these words as such and not to represent them by "the death" or "the person."
    The Greek noun used here means "fellowship," "communion," "sharing." In this passage it means to take part in Christ's self-giving, his death. To drink the wine of the Lord's Supper is to take part in his sacrificial death.
    The second rhetorical question, having to do with the loaf of bread, has the same form in Greek as the first question about the cup. The Greek says "Is not the bread we break fellowship with Christ's body?"

| 10.17 TEV | RSV |
|---|---|
| Because there is the one loaf of bread, all of us, though many, are one body, for we all share the same loaf. | Because there is one bread, we who are many are one body, for we all partake of the one bread. |

    the one loaf of bread: literally "one bread." This refers to the small loaf which was broken and distributed among all those taking part in the Supper. The oneness of the loaf symbolizes the oneness of the believers as members of the one Body of Christ, the Church.

The order may be changed: "We are many (people), but we are all one body, because we share the one loaf of bread (in celebrating the Lord's Supper)."
    The beginning of the verse in Greek may be understood differently: "For although we are many, we are all one loaf, one body...." While possible, this wording of the Greek text does not seem very probable.

| 10.18 | TEV | RSV |
|---|---|---|

| | TEV | RSV |
|---|---|---|
| 10.18 | Consider the people of Israel; those who eat what is offered in sacrifice share in the altar's service to God. | Consider the people of Israel;[a] are not those who eat the sacrifices partners in the altar? |

[a]Greek *Israel according to the flesh*

the people of Israel: literally "Israel according to the flesh." Paul means people who are Israelites by race.
    share in the altar's service to God: this translates "are partners of the altar." The argument seems to be as follows: part of the meat was burned on the altar as a sacrifice to God, and part of it was eaten by the worshipers; so, in effect, they became partners with the altar, because they shared in the meat of the animal offered in sacrifice to God. The meaning may be stated as follows: "those who eat part of the sacrifices have fellowship with God, to whom the sacrifice is offered on the altar."

| | TEV | RSV |
|---|---|---|
| 10.19 | Do I imply, then, that an idol or the food offered to it really amounts to anything? | What do I imply then? That food offered to idols is anything, or that an idol is anything? |

Without formally indicating it, Paul switches abruptly from the matter of Jewish sacrifice to pagan sacrifice. Strictly speaking, one would expect him to draw the same conclusion: a person who eats part of the animal which has been sacrificed to an idol (or, pagan god) has fellowship with that idol. Paul, however, does not admit that such a false god really exists; but those who sacrifice to idols believe in the existence of the false gods represented by the idols, and so they have fellowship with those gods. But Paul does not even call them gods—they are really demons.
    The rhetorical question may be represented as a statement, but since the question is answered in verse 20, the form of the question is preferable here. Another translation would be: "Am I implying (or, saying) that an idol is a real god? or that food offered to an idol is a real sacrifice?" The Greek text (see RSV) has first the food and then the idol; it seems easier to understand if the order is reversed, as TEV has done.

| 10.20 TEV | RSV |
|---|---|
| No! What I am saying is that what is sacrificed on pagan altars is offered to demons, not to God. And I do not want you to be partners with demons. | No, I imply that what pagans sacrifice they offer to demons and not to God. I do not want you to be partners with demons. |

The words is offered to demons, not to God (or "is offered to demons and to that which is not God") may be taken as an allusion to Deuteronomy 32.17.

Paul is saying that the gods to whom pagans sacrifice are not really gods but evil demons; and Paul does not want the Corinthian Christians to have fellowship with demons.

| 10.21 TEV | RSV |
|---|---|
| You cannot drink from the Lord's cup and also from the cup of demons; you cannot eat at the Lord's table and also at the table of demons. | You cannot drink the cup of the Lord and the cup of demons. You cannot partake of the table of the Lord and the table of demons. |

You cannot: Paul is not saying that it is physically impossible for a person to eat meat sacrificed to idols and also eat food dedicated to the Lord (the Lord's Supper). He is saying that one excludes the other: whoever has fellowship with the Lord Jesus cannot have fellowship with demons, and vice versa.

It may be difficult to stay with the literal cup and table; so a translation may choose to say "It is impossible for you to drink the wine used in celebrating the Lord's Supper and also to drink wine at a pagan religious celebration; you cannot sit down to celebrate the Lord's Supper and also sit down to a meal in honor of demons."

| 10.22 TEV | RSV |
|---|---|
| Or do we **want** to make the Lord jealous? Do we think that we are stronger than he? | Shall we provoke the Lord to jealousy? Are we stronger than he? |

Or do we want to make the Lord jealous?: this question implies that the Corinthian Christians, or at least some of them, believe that both things can be done, that is, that a believer can take part in the Lord's supper and also in pagan sacrifices.

make the Lord jealous: "provoke the Lord's anger," "defy the Lord." The concept of God's "jealousy" is an Old Testament idea by which is meant God's intense love for his people and his anger at any attempt on their part to share their love and devotion with pagan gods. Such love and devotion should be directed to God alone. See Deuteronomy 4.24; 6.15 where the Hebrew "God is a jealous God" is translated by TEV God... tolerates no rivals.

Do we think...?: the rhetorical question is a denial: "Of course we are not more powerful than he is."

The whole verse may be translated, "If we try to do this we will make the Lord jealous. And we know that we are not stronger than he is."

10.23  TEV

"We are allowed to do anything," so they say. That is true, but not everything is good. "We are allowed to do anything"—but not everything is helpful.

RSV

"All things are lawful," but not all things are helpful. "All things are lawful," but not all things build up.

This is a good place to begin a new section (10.23—11.1), which can have as a heading, "Final Statement of Principles," "Everything Should Be Done for God's Glory," "Show Love and Respect for Your Fellow Believers."

The glory of God and the spiritual well-being of fellow Christians should guide every believer in the decisions he or she makes.

It seems quite clear that the opening words of both parts of this verse (as in 6.12) are claims made by people whose attitude Paul is criticizing. So TEV, RSV, and other translations make this quite explicit; the words are not Paul's but someone else's.

"We are allowed to do anything": "Everything is lawful (or, permitted)," "Nothing is forbidden."

they say: this is an impersonal way of speaking; they means "people," "someone."

is good: "is useful," "helps others."

is helpful: or "helps build one's faith," "strengthens the fellowship," or "is helpful to the Lord's people." The Greek verb "build up" (see RSV) most naturally applies to a group and not simply to an individual. In both instances Paul is talking about the effect of one's actions on other believers.

10.24  TEV

No one should be looking out for his own interests, but for the interests of others.

RSV

Let no one seek his own good, but the good of his neighbor.

This rule applies to Christians: "No believer should do what benefits only himself; he should do what benefits his fellow believers."

10.25  TEV

You are free to eat anything sold in the meat market, without asking any questions because of your conscience.

RSV

Eat whatever is sold in the meat market without raising any question on the ground of conscience.

anything sold in the meat market: this refers specifically to meat left over from pagan sacrifices and which was put on sale in public markets (see introduction to chapter 8). The meaning may be expressed "... to eat any meat sold in the market."

[ 99 ]

<u>without asking any questions because of your conscience</u>: or, as a complete sentence: "Matters of conscience need not trouble you" or "You need not have any doubts about doing this because of your conscience." Or else, "It is not necessary, for the sake of your conscience, to ask where the meat came from."

For <u>conscience</u> see 8.7,10.

10.26  TEV           RSV

| TEV | RSV |
|---|---|
| For, as the scripture says, "The earth and everything in it belong to the Lord." | For "the earth is the Lord's, and everything in it." |

In support of his statement Paul quotes Psalm 24.1. In the quotation <u>the Lord</u> is God. Everything in the world belongs to God; so that includes the meat that has been offered in sacrifice to an idol.

10.27  TEV           RSV

| TEV | RSV |
|---|---|
| If an unbeliever invites you to a meal and you decide to go, eat what is set before you, without asking any questions because of your conscience. | If one of the unbelievers invites you to dinner and you are disposed to go, eat whatever is set before you without raising any question on the ground of conscience. |

Paul says a Christian is allowed to eat a meal at the home of an unbeliever and not have any hesitation about the food he eats there. The second part of the verse may be translated in the form of a complete sentence: "Don't ask him any questions about the food (or, where the food came from) just because your conscience tells you that it is wrong to eat that food," or "Don't hesitate to eat that food because your conscience begins to hurt."

10.28  TEV           RSV

| TEV | RSV |
|---|---|
| But if someone tells you, "This food was offered to idols," then do not eat that food, for the sake of the one who told you and for con- science' sake— | (But if some one says to you, "This has been offered in sacrifice," then out of consideration for the man who' informed you, and for con- science' sake— |

It is to be noticed that RSV places verses 28-29a within parentheses, thus joining the question in verse 29b directly to verse 27. On this, see below at verse 29b.

 <u>someone</u>: it is not clear who this person is, but most probably he is another Christian, also invited to the meal.

 <u>This food</u>: or "This meat," and "That meat" (in the place of <u>that food</u>).

 <u>was offered to idols</u>: literally "was offered in sacrifice"; but the context makes it clear that pagan sacrifice is meant.

 <u>for the sake of</u>: "out of consideration for," "to spare the feelings of."

Textual Note: some late manuscripts add here the psalm verse quoted in verse 26 (see KJV); this is clearly not part of the original text.

10.29      TEV
that is, not your own conscience, but the other person's conscience.
    "Well, then," someone asks, "why should my freedom to act be limited by another person's conscience?

           RSV
I mean his conscience, not yours — do not eat it.) For why should my liberty be determined by another man's scruples?

Paul makes clear that the words in verse 28 for conscience' sake refer to the conscience of the other person, not the person to whom he is directing the statement.
    Verses 29b-30 are an objection made by someone who has a strong conscience, that is, a believer who knows he is not sinning if he eats food sacrificed to idols. RSV, by placing verses 28-29a within parentheses, makes the words in verses 29b-30 Paul's words, in support of his advice in verse 27 that a Christian has the right to eat food sacrificed to idols—there is no sin in that. TEV and other translations take the words in verses 29b-30 to be those either of someone else or of the person to whom Paul is writing. So, either someone asks or else "you ask." why should my freedom to act be limited by another person's conscience?: "why should a person (or, fellow believer) with a weak conscience be able to restrict my freedom?" or as a statement, "a person who has a weak conscience should not restrict my freedom" or "...should not keep me from doing what I know is right."

10.30      TEV
If I thank God for my food, why should anyone criticize me about food for which I give thanks?"

           RSV
If I partake with thankfulness, why am I denounced because of that for which I give thanks?

If I thank God for my food: or "If I thank God for the food I eat." The Greek verb translated "partake" (RSV) means here "to take part in a meal." The verse may be translated in the form of a statement: "No one has the right to condemn me for eating food for which I have given thanks to God."

10.31      TEV
    Well, whatever you do, whether you eat or drink, do it all for God's glory.

           RSV
    So, whether you eat or drink, or whatever you do, do all to the glory of God.

Paul states a general principle which applies to all Christians, the ones with a strong conscience as well as the ones with a weak conscience.
    for God's glory: "so that people will honor God," "so that God will be regarded as great by everyone."

| 10.32 TEV | RSV |
|---|---|
| Live in such a way as to cause no trouble either to Jews or Gentiles or to the church of God. | Give no offense to Jews or to Greeks or to the church of God, |

as to cause no trouble: the trouble here spoken of is of a spiritual nature; "so as not to offend." Or else, "Don't let your conduct cause anyone to sin."

the church of God: see 1.2.

| 10.33 TEV | RSV |
|---|---|
| Just do as I do; I try to please everyone in all that I do, not thinking of my own good, but of the good of all, so that they might be saved. | just as I try to please all men in everything I do, not seeking my own advantage, but that of many, that they may be saved. |

Paul uses his own conduct as an example for them (see 9.19-23). He does not seek his own welfare, his own convenience, his own rights—he thinks always of the welfare of his fellow believers.

# Chapter 11

11.1      TEV

Imitate me, then, just as I imitate Christ.

      RSV

Be imitators of me, as I am of Christ.

The verse may be translated: "Follow my example, as I follow Christ's example," "Do as I do, just as I do what Christ did."

SECTION HEADING

Covering the Head in Worship: "The Behavior of Women in Public Worship."

From 11.2 to 14.40 Paul takes up various matters having to do with worship. The major part of this longer section (12.1—14.40) is concerned with gifts from the Holy Spirit.

In this section (11.2-16) Paul writes about the conduct of women in public worship, particularly the matter of their covering the head.

11.2      TEV

I praise you because you always remember me and follow the teachings that I have handed on to you.

      RSV

I commend you because you remember me in everything and maintain the traditions even as I have delivered them to you.

Paul begins by praising his readers for remembering him and faithfully obeying the teachings he had transmitted to them.

always remember me: this has to do specifically with Paul's own conduct as a Christian and his teaching.

follow the teachings: or "hold fast to the teachings." The word teachings translates the Greek "traditions," which means a body of information or instructions received from the past and passed on to others. By the use of this word Paul says he had passed on to the Corinthians the Christian teachings he had received from others (see particularly 11.23).

11.3      TEV

But I want you to understand that Christ is supreme over every man, the husband is supreme over his wife, and God is supreme over Christ.

      RSV

But I want you to understand that the head of every man is Christ, the head of a woman is her husband, and the head of Christ is God.

But: this indicates that in what follows, the Corinthian Christians were not following what Paul had taught them.

is supreme: this expression (used three times) translates the Greek noun "head," meaning here "rules over," "has authority over," "is chief of." Paul says that the same relationship exists between Christ and a man as exists between God and Christ, and a man and his wife.

the husband is supreme over his wife: or "man is supreme over woman." The broader meaning is perhaps preferable; but some translations, like TEV and RSV, take the words here in a more restricted sense.

| 11.4 | TEV | RSV |
|---|---|---|
| So a man who prays or proclaims God's message in public worship with his head covered disgraces Christ. | | Any man who prays or prophesies with his head covered dishonors his head, |

a man: Paul is talking about Christian worship, so a man refers to "a Christian man." TEV adds in public worship to avoid the wrong idea that private praying is meant.

proclaims God's message: this translates the Greek verb "to prophesy." In English "to prophesy" has come to mean "to predict," so a word or phrase must be used which is true to the meaning of the original. A prophet was one who proclaimed God's message to the people. Other translations here are "proclaims the message received from God," "speaks in God's name," "transmits God's message." Some English translations use "preach," which may be adequate if it is not understood in the too narrow sense of delivering a formal message in a church building.

disgraces Christ: this translates "disgraces his head." But here it is obvious that "his head" is not used in the normal sense but in the specialized sense of "chief, ruler," as it is in verse 3; so here it means Christ. Some translations have "dishonors Christ, his head." For a man to cover his head was to acknowledge his inferiority to someone present; doing this in worship would mean (as Paul sees it) to acknowledge that there was some other man there who was his superior, and thus would be to disgrace Christ, the only one who is superior to man.

| 11.5 | TEV | RSV |
|---|---|---|
| And any woman who prays or proclaims God's message in public worship with nothing on her head disgraces her husband; there is no difference between her and a woman whose head has been shaved. | | but any woman who prays or prophesies with her head unveiled dishonors her head—it is the same as if her head were shaven. |

with nothing on her head: "with uncovered head," "without a veil on." A veil was the sign of a woman's subjection to her husband; she always wore it in public and only uncovered her features at home. By refusing to wear the veil in public she brought shame on her husband.

disgraces her husband: the same applies here to the Greek "disgraces her head" as in verse 4; here the woman's "head" is her husband; some translations have "dishonors her husband, who is her head."

a woman whose head has been shaved: this would apply either to a slave or to a woman who indulged in loose living. Probably the latter is implied here.

11.6   TEV

If the woman does not cover her head, she might as well cut her hair. And since it is a shameful thing for a woman to shave her head or cut her hair, she should cover her head.

          RSV

For if a woman will not veil herself, then she should cut off her hair; but if it is disgraceful for a woman to be shorn or shaven, let her wear a veil.

  she might as well cut her hair: this translates the imperative "let her cut her hair." Paul is being ironic, and TEV tries to bring this out by translating she might as well.
  shave her head: this was done with a razor.
  cut her hair: this was done with scissors.


11.7   TEV

A man has no need to cover his head, because he reflects the image and glory of God. But woman reflects the glory of man;

          RSV

For a man ought not to cover his head, since he is the image and glory of God; but woman is the glory of man.

  Man reflects the image and glory of God, who is invisible, and that is why a man does not need to cover his head.
  reflects the image and glory: this translates "is the image and glory." By image is meant the visible representation of some living being; "likeness." This statement reflects Genesis 1.26; 5.1. Glory is the visible manifestation of the nature of God. A better translation would be "man is made in God's likeness, and he reflects God's glory."
  In the same way that man, as subordinate to God, reflects his glory, so woman, as man's subordinate, reflects man's glory. Either "majesty" or "power" or "greatness" might serve as translations of the Greek word.


11.8   TEV

for man was not created from woman, but woman from man.

          RSV

(For man was not made from woman, but woman from man.

  The creation story (Gen 2.21-23) places woman in a subordinate status; she was formed out of the man's rib.


11.9   TEV

Nor was man created for woman's sake, but woman was created for man's sake.

          RSV

Neither was man created for woman, but woman for man.)

  The same creation story (see Gen 2.18) states that woman was created for man's benefit, to meet his needs, and not vice versa. This again shows that she is inferior to man.

| 11.10 TEV | RSV |
|---|---|
| On account of the angels, then, a woman should have a covering over her head to show that she is under her husband's authority. | That is why a woman ought to have a veil[r] on her head, because of the angels. |
| | [r]Greek *authority* (the veil being a symbol of this) |

This verse in Greek begins with the phrase "On this account," which TEV refers to what follows (On account of the angels). But it probably refers back to the preceding statements about woman's subordination to man, and the translation should reflect this: "For this reason," "And so," "This is why," "On account of this."

On account of the angels: it is not certain whether Paul is talking about God's angels, who were thought to be present at Christian worship, or evil angels, who would lust after women with uncovered heads. Probably the former is meant, but given the impossibility of being certain about this, it seems better to translate simply "because of the angels."

Since the verse in Greek has "on this account" at the beginning and "on account of the angels" at the end, it is better to translate: "That (or, This) is why a woman ought to wear a veil as a sign of her husband's authority over her; and she should do it also because of the angels."

a woman should have a covering over her head to show that she is under her husband's authority: this translates the Greek "a woman should have authority upon her head." The Greek word for "authority" is used here in the sense of "a sign (or, indication) of authority"—that is, her husband's authority over her; the meaning could be expressed by saying "a covering over her head as a sign of her subordination (or, dependence)."

| 11.11 TEV | RSV |
|---|---|
| In our life in the Lord, however, woman is not independent of man, nor is man independent of woman. | (Nevertheless, in the Lord woman is not independent of man nor man of woman; |

In our life in the Lord: a better translation would be "As we live in union with the Lord" (see 1.2). Or else "As believers" or "In our Christian life."

is not independent: the negative may be stated positively: "man is just as important (or, essential) to woman as woman is essential to man."

| 11.12 TEV | RSV |
|---|---|
| For as woman was made from man, in the same way man is born of woman; and it is God who brings everything into existence. | for as woman was made from man, so man is now born of woman. And all things are from God.) |

woman was made from man: another reference to the creation story (Gen 2.21-23); perhaps here it would be well to say "the first woman was made from (the first) man."

in the same way: this modifies the whole preceding statement; but it could be taken to mean that man is born of woman in the same way that the first woman was made from man. Perhaps it would be better to balance the two clauses by saying "For even as...so also...."

man is born of woman: this refers to the natural process of generation. RSV has "man is now born of woman" in order to make clear that this is not a reference to the creation account. This is useful and should be imitated in other translations.

it is God who brings everything into existence: this translates "all things are from God"—including men and women both. "God is the creator of all," "everything owes its existence to God."

| 11.13 | TEV | RSV |
|---|---|---|
| | Judge for yourselves whether it is proper for a woman to pray to God in public worship with nothing on her head. | Judge for yourselves; is it proper for a woman to pray to God with her head uncovered? |

Paul appeals to the Corinthians' sense of decency: whether it is proper (or, "fitting" or "seemly"). The Greek is in the form of a question: "Is it proper...?" Paul expects them to say "No" but leaves it to them to answer. TEV again adds in public worship to make clear that Paul is not talking about private prayer.

| 11.14 | TEV | RSV |
|---|---|---|
| | Why, nature itself teaches you that long hair on a man is a disgrace, | Does not nature itself teach you that for a man to wear long hair is degrading to him, |

nature itself: Paul appeals to the natural order of creation. It was not universal custom at that time for men to keep their hair real short. In any case, Paul would be talking about a man never cutting his hair and letting it grow long, as women let their hair grow. Paul sees here a principle operating in the natural order of things. It may be difficult to express the concept of nature itself: "the way things are," "the way things are done." Since Paul would not think of nature as being independent of God, the meaning may be expressed by "the way God created the world."

| 11.15 | TEV | RSV |
|---|---|---|
| | but on a woman it is a thing of beauty. Her long hair has been given her to serve as a covering. | but if a woman has long hair, it is her pride? For her hair is given to her for a covering. |

a thing of beauty: literally "glory" as the opposite of disgrace in the previous verse; the contrast may be established by saying "dishonorable...honorable," "shame...honor," "a reason for shame...a reason for pride."

has been given her: by God, that is.

to serve as a covering: or "in the place of a veil."

| 11.16　　　TEV | RSV |
|---|---|
| But if anyone wants to argue about it, all I have to say is that neither we nor the churches of God have any other custom in worship. | If any one is disposed to be contentious, we recognize no other practice, nor do the churches of God. |

Paul appeals finally to <u>custom in worship</u> which prevails in the churches and which he and his <u>colleagues approve</u> of.

<u>wants to argue</u>: "is inclined to contest (or, to oppose)."

<u>the churches of God</u>: here, as in 10.32 (<u>the church of God</u>), a difficulty might arise since the expression seems to imply that there are churches which are not of God. Paul is talking about Christian congregations, so it might be better to represent the Greek by "Christian churches" or else "churches which worship God."

<u>we</u>: this probably means Paul and the other apostles; or else it might be a way of saying Paul himself.


SECTION HEADING

The Lord's Supper

In this section (11.17-34) Paul deals first with the abuses which were taking place in the celebration of the Lord's Supper at the church in Corinth (verses 17-22); then he reports the tradition he had received about how the Lord Jesus instituted the Supper (verses 23-26), and closes the section with instructions and warnings (verses 27-34).


| 11.17　　　TEV | RSV |
|---|---|
| In the following instructions, however, I do not praise you, because your meetings for worship actually do more harm than good. | But in the following instructions I do not commend you, because when you come together it is not for the better but for the worse. |

<u>I do not praise you</u>: this is in contrast with the praise he had expressed in verse 2.

<u>your meetings for worship</u>: this translates "(when) you assemble."

<u>do more harm than good</u>: "make things worse, not better."

The verse may be translated: "In what I say to you now, however, I do not praise you. This is because your worship services do not make you better Christians but worse."


| 11.18　　　TEV | RSV |
|---|---|
| In the first place, I have been told that there are opposing groups in your meetings; and this I believe is partly true. | For, in the first place, when you assemble as a church, I hear that there are divisions among you; and I partly believe it, |

<u>I have been told</u>: probably by members of Chloe's family (see 1.11).

<u>opposing groups</u>: the same Greek word is translated <u>divisions</u> in 1.10; "factions."

in your meetings: or "when you gather as a church."
and this I believe is partly true: "I believe that there is some truth to this," "I believe this report is not completely wrong."

11.19          TEV                              RSV
(No doubt there must be divisions      for there must be factions among
among you so that the ones who are     you in order that those who are
in the right may be clearly seen.)     genuine among you may be recog-
                                       nized.

Paul here says that opposing groups in the church are not only unavoidable but necessary. This seems to be irony on Paul's part, so TEV has expressed this by No doubt there must be.
divisions: this translates a word found only here in 1 Corinthians: "factions," "mutually exclusive groups."
the ones who are in the right: "the people who are approved by God," "those who are genuine believers."
may be clearly seen: "may be known (or, recognized)," "may show up." Or else the whole conclusion may be stated, "so that you can clearly see which people are in the right."

11.20          TEV                              RSV
When you meet together as a group,     When you meet together, it is not
it is not the Lord's Supper that       the Lord's supper that you eat.
you eat.

it is not the Lord's Supper that you eat: Paul means by this that although the Corinthian Christians maintained that they did meet in order to celebrate the Lord's Supper, their conduct was such as to make of the occasion something quite different. The meaning may be expressed by "the meal you eat is something else; it is not really the Lord's Supper."

11.21          TEV                              RSV
For as you eat, each one goes ahead    For in eating, each one goes ahead
with his own meal, so that some are    with his own meal, and one is hun-
hungry while others get drunk.         gry and another is drunk.

each one goes ahead with his own meal: or "you don't wait for one another before you start eating," or "you start eating before everybody gets there." This appears to mean that each family group brought its own food and would start eating before the others had arrived; but there would be more point to what Paul is saying if the food for the meal was provided for from the group's funds, and that the early arrivals would eat most or all the food before everybody arrived.
meal: at that time the Lord's Supper was celebrated at the close of a regular meal eaten in common by the worshipers (in time this meal came to be known as the *agape*, the love feast). It should be constantly borne in mind that the Christians assembled in private homes; there were no church buildings at that time.

| 11.22 TEV | RSV |
|---|---|
| Don't you have your own homes in which to eat and drink? Or would you rather despise the church of God and put to shame the people who are in need? What do you expect me to say to you about this? Shall I praise you? Of course I don't! | What! Do you not have houses to eat and drink in? Or do you despise the church of God and humiliate those who have nothing? What shall I say to you? Shall I commend you in this? No, I will not. |

Paul rebukes them sharply. Such feasting should be done at home.

TEV translates the verse with four questions and a closing affirmation (following the form of the Greek). Another way would be "You have your own homes in which to eat and drink. So you should not act like this at your meetings, for this shows that you despise the church of God and humiliate your needy fellow believers. Don't expect any praise on this matter; I certainly do not praise you."

the church of God: see verse 16.

| 11.23 TEV | RSV |
|---|---|
| For I received from the Lord the teaching that I passed on to you: that the Lord Jesus, on the night he was betrayed, took a piece of bread, | For I received from the Lord what I also delivered to you, that the Lord Jesus on the night when he was betrayed took bread, |

To show up even more strongly the abuses in Corinth in the celebration of the Lord's Supper, Paul gives an account of the tradition he had received as to how the Supper was instituted.

I received from the Lord: the words, both in English and in Greek, imply that the Lord Jesus had personally told Paul about the Supper. It is highly improbable that this was so, but a translation should not try to give the impression that Paul had received the tradition at second hand.

the teaching: "the information," "the report," "the tradition."

betrayed: thus understood, this refers specifically to Judas' betrayal of Jesus. The Greek verb used here means "to hand over" (to the authorities); it is used of Judas' action (see Mark 3.19; 14.10,11,18, 21,42,44). Here either betrayed or "handed over to the authorities" could be used. If the passive form of the verb cannot be used, "when Judas betrayed him" or "when Judas turned him over to the authorities." The translation should make it clear that Jesus instituted the Supper before being betrayed by Judas in the Garden of Gethsemane.

a piece of bread: better, "a loaf of bread" (see 10.17).

| 11.24 TEV | RSV |
|---|---|
| gave thanks to God, broke it, and said, "This is my body, which is for you. Do this in memory of me." | and when he had given thanks, he broke it, and said, "This is my body which is for[8] you. Do this in remembrance of me."

[8]Other ancient authorities read *broken for* |

broke it: "broke it into pieces."

and said: "and said to his disciples."

This is my body: given the use of these words in the Christian community as a whole, it is better to translate them quite literally, and not "this represents (or, symbolizes) my body."

which is for you: there is no verb in the best Greek text of this clause; some Greek manuscripts have "which is broken for you," and many ancient versions have "which is given (or, betrayed) for you." If a verb is needed, the translation could be "which is given for you."

Do this: "Eat this bread."

in memory of me: "so that you will not forget me," "to remember what I have done."

---

| 11.25 TEV | RSV |
|---|---|
| In the same way, after the supper he took the cup and said, "This cup is God's new covenant, sealed with my blood. Whenever you drink it, do so in memory of me." | In the same way also the cup, after supper, saying, "This cup is the new covenant in my blood. Do this, as often as you drink it, in remembrance of me." |

In the same way: or "Also," "Likewise." The words may imply that a prayer of thanksgiving was offered also for the wine.

after the supper: "after they had finished the meal."

the cup: "the cup of wine."

This cup is: here cup stands for the wine in it; perhaps "This cup of wine" would be the best way to express the meaning.

God's new covenant: the Greek is "the new covenant." The words recall God's original covenant with his people, made at Mount Sinai; this is the new covenant ("agreement, accord, pact") with his people.

sealed with my blood: this translates what is literally "in my blood." In the Old Testament the blood of a sacrificed animal made the covenant binding (see Exo 24.7-8); here it is Christ's blood, poured out in his death, which seals, or ratifies, the covenant.

Whenever you drink it: that is, the wine in the cup. So it is better to have "he took the cup of wine" at the beginning of the verse, so that it here refers back to the wine as such.

---

| 11.26 TEV | RSV |
|---|---|
| This means that every time you eat this bread and drink from this cup you proclaim the Lord's death until he comes. | For as often as you eat this bread and drink the cup, you proclaim the Lord's death until he comes. |

These words are by Paul, and a device such as TEV This means that should be used so that the reader and the listeners will be aware of the fact that the speaker here is not Jesus himself.

eat this bread and drink from this cup: it should not appear that Paul is talking about the very loaf of bread that Jesus broke or the very cup of wine that he offered his disciples. So it might be better to translate "whenever you eat the bread and drink the wine of the Lord's Supper" or "whenever you celebrate the Lord's Supper."

proclaim: by its very nature proclaim is oral, that is, it means spoken words; but Paul means that the celebration of the Supper is itself a "proclamation," an announcement. Perhaps a verb that does not imply spoken words may be used: "you are making known."

until he comes: TEV could be read as though until he comes modifies the Lord's death; it is better, therefore, to change the order: "And so, until the Lord comes, you will be proclaiming his death every time you ...."

| 11.27 TEV | RSV |
|---|---|
| It follows that if anyone eats the Lord's bread or drinks from his cup in a way that dishonors him, he is guilty of sin against the Lord's body and blood. | Whoever, therefore, eats the bread or drinks the cup of the Lord in an unworthy manner will be guilty of profaning the body and blood of the Lord. |

the Lord's bread...his cup: again, it should not appear that this means the loaf of bread the Lord broke or the cup he offered; so it may be better to say, "if anyone celebrates the Lord's Supper in a way...."

in a way that dishonors him: this refers specifically to what was happening in Corinth (verses 18-22). The Lord's name was being profaned by the way in which they were celebrating the Supper.

he is guilty of sin against: "he sins against," "he profanes," "he brings disgrace on." The underlying idea is that "the body and the blood of the Lord" is sacred and must be treated in a reverent manner. It is uncertain whether by "the body and the blood of the Lord" Paul means the elements of the Supper (the bread and the wine) or the actual death of Jesus, which the Supper celebrates.

| 11.28 TEV | RSV |
|---|---|
| So then, everyone should examine himself first, and then eat the bread and drink from the cup. | Let a man examine himself, and so eat of the bread and drink of the cup. |

examine himself: "examine his motives," "examine his conscience (or, heart)." Such an examination, of course, is not simply in order to obtain information; it implies the elimination of any unworthy motive or thought.

| 11.29 TEV | RSV |
|---|---|
| For if he does not recognize the meaning of the Lord's body when he eats the bread and drinks from the cup, he brings judgment on himself as he eats and drinks. | For any one who eats and drinks without discerning the body eats and drinks judgment upon himself. |

if he does not recognize the meaning of the Lord's body: this translates the Greek "if he does not discern the body." What seems to be implied is "if he does not recognize that the cup and the bread represent the Lord's body." But it is impossible to say what Paul meant here by the Lord's body: (1) the church, (2) the Supper, or (3) the physical body of Jesus, which had been offered in sacrifice to God. The most probable interpretation seems to be "if he does not recognize that the bread and wine represent the Lord's self-sacrifice for us."

he brings judgment on himself: "he will be punished by God."

Another way of translating the verse may be "Whenever someone eats the bread and drinks the wine of the Lord's Supper, he must recognize that the bread and the wine represent the Lord's sacrificial death. If he doesn't, he will be punished by God."

Textual Notes: many Greek manuscripts add "in an unworthy manner" (as in verse 27); see KJV. This is not part of the original text. The Greek text has "the body"; many manuscripts add "of the Lord," an explanatory addition. TEV the Lord's body represents the meaning of the Greek "the body."

11.30  TEV

That is why many of you are sick and weak, and several have died.

RSV

That is why many of you are weak and ill, and some have died.[t]

[t]Greek *have fallen asleep* (as in 15.6,20)

That is why: this refers back to God's judgment spoken of in the previous verses.

have died: this translates the Greek "have fallen asleep," a common way of speaking about dying.

11.31  TEV

If we would examine ourselves first, we would not come under God's judgment.

RSV

But if we judged ourselves truly, we should not be judged.

examine ourselves: as in verse 28.

first: before celebrating the Supper.

The order of the clauses may be reversed: "But God would not punish us (like this) if we were to examine our motives before celebrating the Lord's Supper."

11.32  TEV

But we are judged and punished by the Lord, so that we shall not be condemned together with the world.

RSV

But when we are judged by the Lord, we are chastened[u] so that we may not be condemned along with the world.

[u]Or *when we are judged we are being chastened by the Lord*

Paul sees God's judgment on the believers as a disciplinary measure, in order to keep them from being condemned with nonbelievers. The meaning may be expressed: "But the Lord judges us and punishes (or, disciplines) us, so that we will not be condemned with nonbelievers."

| 11.33 | TEV | RSV |
|---|---|---|

| TEV | RSV |
|---|---|
| So then, my brothers, when you gather together to eat the Lord's Supper, wait for one another. | So then, my brethren, when you come together to eat, wait for one another— |

my brothers: see 1.10.

Paul concludes his instructions advising the Corinthian Christians to wait for one another when they gather to celebrate the Supper (see verses 20-21).

| 11.34 | TEV | RSV |
|---|---|---|

| TEV | RSV |
|---|---|
| And if anyone is hungry, he should eat at home, so that you will not come under God's judgment as you meet together. As for the other matters, I will settle them when I come. | if any one is hungry, let him eat at home—lest you come together to be condemned. About the other things I will give directions when I come. |

RSV is probably correct in placing "if any one is hungry, let him eat at home" within dashes, as a parenthetical remark, thus joining "lest you come together to be condemned" with verse 33. In TEV style, this can be achieved by joining so that you will not come under God's judgment as you meet together (verse 34) directly to the end of verse 33 (which would end with a comma, not a period). The words And if anyone is hungry, he should eat at home would come next, perhaps within parentheses.

the other matters: or "the other details"; probably, but not necessarily, these have to do with the celebration of the Supper.

I will settle them: "I will dispose of them," "I will tell you what to do about them."

I come: or "I go there."

# Chapter 12

Gifts from the Holy Spirit: "Spiritual Gifts."
Paul's discussion of this matter goes from 12.1 to 14.40. Of course
it is the gift of "speaking in tongues" that takes up more space, but it
should be noticed that love, the subject of chapter 13, is dealt with in
this context of gifts from the Holy Spirit. Paul has already referred to
the subject (see 2.13-14).

| 12.1 TEV | RSV |
|---|---|
| Now, concerning what you wrote about the gifts from the Holy Spirit.<br><br>I want you to know the truth about them, my brothers. | Now concerning spiritual gifts,$^x$ brethren, I do not want you to be uninformed.<br><br>$^x$Or *spiritual persons* |

Now, concerning what you wrote: see 7.1.
the gifts from the Holy Spirit: this translates the Greek "the spiritual things" (if the Greek is taken to be neuter; as RSV footnote indicates, it may be taken as masculine "spiritual persons," but this seems
unlikely). The simple "gifts of the Spirit" could be misunderstood; it
is better to translate "the gifts that the Holy Spirit bestows on Christians."
I want you to know the truth about them: TEV phrases positively
what in Greek is a negative statement: "I don't want you to be ignorant
(about them)."
brothers: see 1.10.

| 12.2 TEV | RSV |
|---|---|
| You know that while you were still heathen, you were led astray in many ways to the worship of life-less idols. | You know that when you were hea-then, you were led astray to dumb idols, however you may have been moved. |

heathen: "non-Christians"; "before you became Christians."
led astray in many ways: the Greek verb translated led astray may
be understood to imply the effect of an overpowering force; here most
likely it refers to the frenzied practices and orgies which were part
of many pagan religions. "You were seized by powerful forces (or, im-
pulses)."
lifeless idols: the biblical phrase "dumb idols" (that is, idols
that cannot speak) is a way of describing them as powerless, ineffective,
dead, nonexistent. So it might be better to say "dead gods" or "gods that
really do not exist."

| 12.3 TEV | RSV |
|---|---|
| I want you to know that no one who is led by God's Spirit can say "A curse on Jesus!" and no one can confess "Jesus is Lord," unless he is guided by the Holy Spirit. | Therefore I want you to understand that no one speaking by the Spirit of God ever says "Jesus be cursed!" and no one can say "Jesus is Lord" except by the Holy Spirit. |

This verse talks about two "inspired" confessions: (1) A curse on Jesus, or "Jesus is accursed," "Jesus be damned." Paul is saying that this could not be said by someone who was under the influence of the Spirit of God; whoever said that was under the influence of an evil spirit, or demon. It is not clear where and under what circumstances someone would say A curse on Jesus! (2) The opposite "Jesus is Lord" was the confession of someone under the influence of the Holy Spirit. Instead of the double negative no one...unless, it might be better to restructure the verse as follows: "A person who is led by God's Spirit cannot say 'A curse on Jesus,' and a person can say 'Jesus is Lord' only if he is guided by the Holy Spirit."

| 12.4-5 TEV | RSV |
|---|---|
| There are different kinds of spiritual gifts, but the same Spirit gives them. 5 There are different ways of serving, but the same Lord is served. | Now there are varieties of gifts, but the same Spirit; 5 and there are varieties of service, but the same Lord; |

Verses 4-6 form one sentence in Greek; in all three verses there is the same structure: "the same Spirit...the same Lord...the same God" (in verse 6 a qualifying statement is added). TEV has made explicit what seems to be implicit in the text, the same Spirit gives them (verse 4) and the same Lord is served (verse 5).

spiritual gifts are gifts given by the Holy Spirit (see verse 1).

Lord: a title for Jesus. Instead of the passive is served, an active form may be better: "but all (or, we all) serve the same Lord (Jesus)."

| 12.6 TEV | RSV |
|---|---|
| There are different abilities to perform service, but the same God gives ability to everyone for their particular service. | and there are varieties of working, but it is the same God who inspires them all in every one. |

abilities to perform service: this translates the one Greek word "works," "services," almost synonymous with the noun in verse 5 (which RSV translates "service"). Here, however, it is the power or capacity to perform these various tasks that is meant.

| 12.7　　　　TEV | RSV |
|---|---|
| The Spirit's presence is shown in some way in each person for the good of all. | To each is given the manifestation of the Spirit for the common good. |

The Spirit's presence is shown: this translates "the manifestation of the Spirit" (RSV); an active form may be preferred, "God gives everyone some proof of the Spirit's presence." This "proof," of course, is the gift.

the good of all: that is, the whole Christian community. The gift from the Spirit is not for the benefit of the person who receives it.

| 12.8-9　　　　TEV | RSV |
|---|---|
| The Spirit gives one person a message full of wisdom, while to another person the same Spirit gives a message full of knowledge. 9 One and the same Spirit gives faith to one person, while to another person he gives the power to heal. | To one is given through the Spirit the utterance of wisdom, and to another the utterance of knowledge according to the same Spirit, 9 to another faith by the same Spirit, to another gifts of healing by the one Spirit, |

In verses 8-10 Paul lists the various gifts from the Holy Spirit. The point he emphasizes is that all these various spiritual abilities are gifts that are received, and all are given by one and the same Spirit of God.

a message full of wisdom: it is not clear how this differs from the next gift, a message full of knowledge. It should be noticed that in the large majority of instances Paul uses "wisdom" and "knowledge" in this letter in a negative sense: merely human wisdom as opposed to God's wisdom, and false knowledge as opposed to true knowledge. In 2.7, however, he speaks of God's secret wisdom that he, Paul, proclaims; and in 1.5 Paul congratulates his readers for being rich in...all knowledge.

faith: this does not seem to be saving faith in Christ (which, by definition, every Christian has), but a special faith, probably the faith to work miracles. But it should be noticed that Paul makes explicit mention of this gift in verse 10.

the power to heal: it may be necessary to add the object, "sick people."

| 12.10　　　　TEV | RSV |
|---|---|
| The Spirit gives one person the power to work miracles; to another, the gift of speaking God's message; and to yet another, the ability to tell the difference between gifts that come from the Spirit and those that do not. To one person he gives the ability to speak in strange tongues, and to another he gives the ability to explain what is said. | to another the working of miracles, to another prophecy, to another the ability to distinguish between spirits, to another various kinds of tongues, to another the interpretation of tongues. |

miracles: there is usually no difficulty in translating this word (in Greek it is literally "powers," that is, extraordinary powers). Something like "extraordinary happenings," "wonderful deeds," "things that cannot be understood (or, explained)." The main component is the impossibility of accomplishing these things unless a person has God's power; these are things that only God himself can do.

speaking God's message: see 11.4.

to tell the difference between gifts that come from the Spirit and those that do not: this translates the noun phrase "differences of spirits." Paul has in mind the various manifestations of "inspired" abilities. Clearly not all of them are from God's Spirit, and the ability to distinguish the genuine gifts from the false ones is itself a gift from God's Spirit. Some translations have simply "the ability to distinguish between false spirits and the true Spirit," but this may suggest a situation which is difficult for the reader to understand.

speak in strange tongues: this translates the gift commonly referred to as "speaking in tongues." It is quite evident, from what Paul says about this gift in this letter and from what is said about it elsewhere, that this gift (technically known as "glossolalia," which is the transliteration of the Greek word which means "speak in tongue[s]") was not that of an intelligible language, but of strange sounds and utterances produced by a deep emotional and spiritual experience. Most translations have "speak in tongue(s)." Others have "to speak with strange words," "to speak a mysterious language," "to speak unknown sounds."

explain what is said: "interpret the speaking in tongues." The ability to understand and explain what is said "in tongues" is itself a gift, not a learned skill.


| 12.11 TEV | RSV |
|---|---|
| But it is one and the same Spirit who does all this; as he wishes, he gives a different gift to each person. | All these are inspired by one and the same Spirit, who apportions to each one individually as he wills. |

one and the same Spirit: this is a common English construction (see its use also in verse 9) to emphasize the identity of the subject. There are other ways of stating this: "The one Spirit (of God) does this," "All this is done by the Spirit of God, and no one else," "The Spirit alone does all this."


SECTION HEADING

One Body with Many Parts: "We All Belong to the Same Body."

In this section (12.12-31) Paul uses the human body as a figure of the church and the relations of Christians with one another as members of Christ's Body. The exposition of how the various members of the one body relate to one another ends at verse 27, and verses 27-31a are the application of the figure to the church.

| 12.12 | TEV | RSV |
|---|---|---|

| Christ is like a single body, which has many parts; it is still one body, even though it is made up of different parts. | For just as the body is one and has many members, and all the members of the body, though many, are one body, so it is with Christ. |
|---|---|

Christ is like a single body: or "Christ is like a body." It may be better to restructure the verse as follows: "A (human) body has many parts, but this does not mean that it is many bodies; it is still one body, with many parts. That is what Christ is like (or, The same is true of Christ)." Paul would be expected to say "So it is with the church," but for Paul the church was in fact Christ's body; the two are not separated. The church is not like a body; it is the Body of Christ.

In verses 12-26 the word translated part is used a number of times. The Greek uses the same word, and so does TEV part(s). RSV has "member," "organ(s)," "part(s)." A word should be used which is general enough to refer to all parts of the body, both the external members and the internal organs. This may be impossible to do; NEB, for example, uses the phrase "limb(s) and organ(s)" three times (verses 12,18,27).

| 12.13 | TEV | RSV |
|---|---|---|

| In the same way, all of us, whether Jews or Gentiles, whether slaves or free, have been baptized into the one body by the same Spirit, and we have all been given the one Spirit to drink. | For by one Spirit we were all baptized into one body—Jews or Greeks, slaves or free—and all were made to drink of one Spirit. |
|---|---|

In the same way: this is said to make clear that Paul now makes the application, and it shows what the statement Christ is like a single body means. So if verse 12 is made to end with "the same is true of Christ," verse 13 may begin "For all of us have been baptized by the same Spirit and so we form one body."

Gentiles: this translates "Greeks;" here, in opposition to "Jews," it is better to say "Gentiles" (see 1.22-23).

have been baptized...by the same Spirit: the figure is a bit strange. The Greek "in the one Spirit" may be taken to mean, as RSV, TEV and others take it, "by the one Spirit," that is, the Spirit does the baptizing; or else the preposition in can be taken as a locative: "we were baptized in the one Spirit" (the Spirit being the element, as water is the element in baptism). It is impossible to be dogmatic; many translations are ambiguous, but those that are clear have either "by the same (or, one) Spirit" or else something like "in baptism we have received the same Spirit" (which departs somewhat radically from the Greek text).

into the one body: it seems more satisfactory to translate "to form one body"; that is, the baptism by (or, in) the one Spirit has as its result the formation of the one body.

The TEV construction of the single sentence in verse 13 is rather complex, and it may be more satisfactory to restructure as follows:

"There are many of us, and we are different: some are Jews, others are Gentiles; some are slaves, others are free. But all of us have been baptized by (or, in) the same Spirit, and so we are one body; and all of us have been given to drink of the one Spirit."

have all been given the one Spirit to drink: Paul seems here to allude to the Lord's Supper as he speaks of the oneness of believers in Christ. If it is better to use the active form of the verb "to give," one may say "God (or, The Spirit) has given us all the one (or, same) Spirit to drink." The metaphor "drink the Spirit" may be impossible or much too difficult in some languages, so it might be necessary to add a phrase like "as it were" or "so to speak" to show that this is a figure of speech. It may be necessary to abandon the figure altogether; if so, "we have been given the same Spirit in our hearts" or something similar might be said.

| 12.14 TEV | RSV |
|---|---|
| For the body itself is not made up of only one part, but of many parts. | For the body does not consist of one member but of many. |

Paul now returns to the figure of a body and its members.

is not made up of: or, more simply, "the body is not just one member (or, part)—it is many members (or, parts)."

| 12.15-16 TEV | RSV |
|---|---|
| If the foot were to say, "Because I am not a hand, I don't belong to the body," that would not keep it from being a part of the body. 16 And if the ear were to say, "Because I am not an eye, I don't belong to the body," that would not keep it from being a part of the body. | If the foot should say, "Because I am not a hand, I do not belong to the body," that would not make it any less a part of the body. 16 And if the ear should say, "Because I am not an eye, I do not belong to the body," that would not make it any less a part of the body. |

In order to avoid the double negative in these two verses, it might be better to restructure as follows: "The foot would still be a part of (or, belong to) the body even if it said, 'I am not a hand, and so I do not belong to the body.' And the ear would still be a part of the body even if it said, 'I am not an eye, and so I am not part of the body.'" Or else: "The foot might say, 'Since I am not a hand, I am not a part of the body.' But that foot would still be a part of the body. The ear might say, 'Since I am not an eye, I am not part of the body.' But that ear would still be a part of the body."

| 12.17-18 TEV | RSV |
|---|---|
| If the whole body were just an eye, how could it hear? And if it were only an ear, how could it smell? | If the whole body were an eye, where would be the hearing? If the whole body were an ear, where |

| | |
|---|---|
| 18 As it is, however, God put every different part in the body just as he wanted it to be. | would be the sense of smell? 18 But as it is, God arranged the organs in the body, each one of them, as he chose. |

The two rhetorical questions in verse 17 can be represented as statements: "The body could not hear if it were just an eye, nor could it smell if it were just an ear." Or, "If the body were just an eye, it could not hear; if it were just an ear, it could not smell."

As it is: "The way things are," "But the fact is that."

every different part: "every member."

| 12.19-20 TEV | RSV |
|---|---|
| There would not be a body if it were all only one part! 20 As it is, there are many parts but one body. | If all were a single organ, where would the body be? 20 As it is, there are many parts, yet one body. |

In verse 19 TEV has represented as a statement what in Greek is a rhetorical question: "If the whole consisted of one part (or, organ), where would the body be?" It seems better to use a statement; for example, "If it were all one part, there would be no body." The body does not exist unless there are different parts joined together in a whole.

As it is: "The fact is" (as in verse 18).

| 12.21 TEV | RSV |
|---|---|
| So then, the eye cannot say to the hand, "I don't need you!" Nor can the head say to the feet, "Well, I don't need you!" | The eye cannot say to the hand, "I have no need of you," nor again the head to the feet, "I have no need of you." |

Returning to his parable of the body, Paul shows that every different part is necessary; the body as a whole cannot get along without its different parts.

cannot say: by this Paul means that it would be false, it would be wrong; actually the eye could "say" to the hand, "I don't need you," but it would be a lie, because the eye does need the hands.

the hand: even though the Greek is singular, it might be well to say "the hands."

| 12.22-24 TEV | RSV |
|---|---|
| On the contrary, we cannot do without the parts of the body that seem to be weaker; 23 and those parts that we think aren't worth very much are the ones which we treat with greater care; while the parts of the body which don't look very nice are treated with special | On the contrary, the parts of the body which seem to be weaker are indispensable, 23 and those parts of the body which we think less honorable we invest with the greater honor, and our unpresentable parts are treated with greater modesty, 24 which our |

modesty, 24 which the more beautiful parts do not need. God himself
has put the body together in such
a way as to give greater honor to
those parts that need it.

more presentable parts do not
require. But God has so composed
the body, giving the greater
honor to the inferior part,

As both TEV and RSV punctuation show, the sentence runs from verse
22 to verse 24a. It is possible to make of verse 22 a complete sentence
and begin a new one with verse 23, or else break up the whole passage
into several sentences.

Paul speaks of three kinds of members, or parts, of the body: (1)
those that seem to be weaker (verse 22); (2) those that we think aren't
worth very much (verse 23a); and (3) those which don't look very nice
(verse 23b). Paul here seems to be thinking more in terms of the church
and its members rather than of the model, the human body. But formally
at least, Paul is still talking about the body as such.

the parts of the body that seem to be weaker: this could easily be
applied to the eyes, which are not "strong," that is, are incapable of
protecting themselves. A translation could say "The weaker they appear, the more indispensable they are."

we think aren't worth very much: or "those parts of the body that
we think are less important." It is uncertain which parts Paul is talking about.

we treat with greater care: or "we dress up more carefully."

which don't look very nice: RSV has "unpresentable parts"; Paul
probably has in mind the genital organs. The translation could be "those
parts which it's not proper to talk about."

put the body together: "fashioned the body," "composed the body."

those parts that need it: "those parts of the body that seem to
lack it."

| 12.25-26 | TEV | RSV |
|---|---|---|

And so there is no division in
the body, but all its different
parts have the same concern for
one another. 26 If one part of
the body suffers, all the other
parts suffer with it; if one part
is praised, all the other parts
share its happiness.

that there may be no discord in
the body, but that the members
may have the same care for one
another. 26 If one member suffers,
all suffer together; if one member is honored, all rejoice together.

In RSV verse 25 follows verse 24 as the purpose; TEV has made it
the result, And so there is no division. The word translated division
(RSV "discord") can be represented as "lack of unity," "opposing
groups," "factions" (see 1.10; 11.18).

the same concern: "the same care" (RSV). Or, "that each part might
be just as concerned for the other parts as it is for itself."

Verse 26 may be restructured as follows: "All the members of the
body suffer when one (member) suffers; all the members rejoice when
one (member) is praised."

| 12.27 | TEV | RSV |
|---|---|---|

<table>
<tr><td>All of you are Christ's body, and each one is a part of it.</td><td>Now you are the body of Christ and individually members of it.</td></tr>
</table>

In verses 27-30a Paul makes the direct application of his figure of speech: "You are all together the body of Christ, and each one individually is a part (or, member) of the body."

| 12.28 | TEV | RSV |
|---|---|---|

<table>
<tr><td>In the church God has put all in place: in the first place apostles, in the second place prophets, and in the third place teachers; then those who perform miracles, followed by those who are given the power to heal or to help others or to direct them or to speak in strange tongues.</td><td>And God has appointed in the church first apostles, second prophets, third teachers, then workers of miracles, then healers, helpers, administrators, speakers in various kinds of tongues.</td></tr>
</table>

Here for the first time Paul uses the word church, since now the application is being made to the various officers and duties in the church.

has put all in place: "has given all members their place." It should be carefully noticed that the text specifically has first, second, third, then, and followed by. This is order of rank or importance, not of time.

apostles: see 1.1. These are not only the twelve disciples of Jesus, but they and others as well (such as Paul himself).

prophets: see 11.4. Here the translation could be "those who proclaim God's message." Care should be taken not to use a word which would make the readers think of Old Testament prophets.

teachers: for further references to this office see Acts 13.1; Romans 12.7; Ephesians 4.11; 2 Timothy 1.11; James 3.1. These would appear to be people who taught the Christian faith, both its history and its rules.

perform miracles: as in verse 10.

the power to heal: as in verse 9.

to help others: it is not clear what this office was, but the word itself suggests the kind of help needy or poor people require.

to direct them: "to guide people," "to instruct people." It is not clear what were the specific duties of these "administrators" (RSV).

to speak in strange tongues: as in verse 10.

| 12.29-30 | TEV |
|---|---|

<table>
<tr><td>They are not all apostles or prophets or teachers. Not everyone has the power to work miracles 30 or to heal diseases or to speak in strange tongues or to explain what is said.</td><td>Are all apostles? Are all prophets? Are all teachers? Do all work miracles? 30 Do all possess gifts of healing? Do all speak with tongues? Do all interpret?</td></tr>
</table>

As RSV shows, these two verses are made up of seven rhetorical questions, all of them expecting the answer "No." TEV has given the meaning in a series of statements. A translation may choose to do it either way, depending on the language. If the form of a question is used, it must be so phrased as to indicate that the expected answer is "No."

| 12.31 | TEV | RSV |
|---|---|---|
| | Set your hearts, then, on the more important gifts.<br><br>    Best of all, however, is the following way. | But earnestly desire the higher gifts.<br><br>    And I will show you a still more excellent way. |

Set your hearts, then, on: "Aspire to," "Desire," "Try to have."
    the more important gifts: "the better gifts," "the more valuable gifts."

    The second part of this verse goes logically with what follows (chapter 13), but most translations keep it as the last part of this section.

    the following way: Paul is talking about love, of course, the subject of chapter 13. Paul does not here explicitly call love a gift from the Spirit. He speaks of it as a way, that is, the rule of the Christian life, which is far superior to all other ways in which the Christian life is lived.

# Chapter 13

SECTION HEADING

Love: "Christian Love."
In this chapter Paul speaks of love as the best way of all for Christians to follow. The chapter divides naturally into three sections: (1) the supremacy of love (verses 1-3); (2) the characteristics of love (verses 4-7); (3) the permanence of love (verses 8-13).

| 13.1 TEV | RSV |
|---|---|
| I may be able to speak the languages of men and even of angels, but if I have no love, my speech is no more than a noisy gong or a clanging bell. | If I speak in the tongues of men and of angels, but have not love, I am a noisy gong or a clanging cymbal. |

the languages of men and even of angels: "all the languages spoken on earth and in heaven." By this phrase Paul includes all languages that exist; he assumes that angels also talk to one another but use a language different from human languages.

if I have no love: "if I do not love others."

my speech is no more than: this translates "I have become" (see RSV). If the translation prefers to keep a figure, perhaps a simile would be better than the metaphor: "I am like...."

a noisy gong or a clanging bell: these two instruments (RSV "gong ...cymbal") are loud but they cannot produce a melody; they are noisy but lack meaning.

| 13.2 TEV | RSV |
|---|---|
| I may have the gift of inspired preaching; I may have all knowledge and understand all secrets; I may have all the faith needed to move mountains—but if I have no love, I am nothing. | And if I have prophetic powers, and understand all mysteries and all knowledge, and if I have all faith, so as to remove mountains, but have not love, I am nothing. |

the gift of inspired preaching: this translates "prophecy" (see 11.4).

have all knowledge and understand all secrets: this reverses the order of the Greek, which has "secrets" first and then "knowledge." The translation may say, "I may know everything; I may understand all mysteries." Here secrets (RSV "mysteries") may refer to God's hidden plans for humanity (see 2.6-7), and some translations have "if I know God's hidden purposes (or, plans)."

I may have all the faith needed: or "My faith in God may be so strong that I can move mountains." This move mountains is most probably said in the sense it appears in Mark 11.23 and Matthew 17.20, referring to prayer or to a direct order that the mountain move. It may be preferable to use a verbal phrase for <u>faith</u>: "I may believe in God so strongly that I can move mountains."

<u>I am nothing</u>: "I am worth nothing," "I amount to nothing."

The verse is structured in such a way that the possibilities <u>I may</u> ...<u>I may</u>...<u>I may</u> are all cited before the qualification <u>but if I have no love</u> is stated. It may be more satisfactory to place <u>the qualifying clause</u> first: "If I have no love, I am worth nothing even if I...."

| 13.3 TEV | RSV |
|---|---|
| I may give away everything I have, and even give up my body to be burned[n]—but if I have no love, this does me no good. | If I give away all I have, and if I deliver my body to be burned,[v] but have not love, I gain nothing. |
| [n]to be burned; *some manuscripts have* in order to boast. | [v]Other ancient authorities read *body that I may glory* |

<u>give away everything I have</u>: this refers to almsgiving, the giving away of one's possessions to help the needy.

<u>give up my body to be burned</u>: this is voluntary martyrdom, the most extreme demonstration of faithfulness and dedication to a cause.

Textual Note: as the RSV and TEV footnoes show, instead of <u>to be burned</u>, many of the oldest and best Greek manuscripts, and some ancient versions, have "in order to boast." The manuscript support for this wording is better than for the one followed by RSV and TEV and most modern translations. The Greek New Testament of the United Bible Societies has "in order to boast" as the text and "to be burned" as a variant in the margin. The principal argument against the best-attested text is that to sacrifice one's life for the purpose of boasting is a matter of pride, and is thereby an act that is not done out of Christian love. Of the better-known modern translations, only Goodspeed follows the best-attested text.

| 13.4-5 TEV | RSV |
|---|---|
| Love is patient and kind; it is not jealous or conceited or proud; 5 love is not ill-mannered or selfish or irritable; love does not keep a record of wrongs; | Love is patient and kind; love is not jealous or boastful; 5 it is not arrogant or rude. Love does not insist on its own way; it is not irritable or resentful; |

In verses 4-7 Paul describes <u>love</u>; it is to be noticed that in Greek all these descriptions are <u>verbs</u> or verbal phrases, not adjectives or noun phrases. Paul's view of love is that it is an active force, not a passive sentiment.

<u>Love is patient</u>: instead of the abstract noun <u>love</u> throughout these verses, it may be preferable to use the verb "to <u>love</u>": "To love means to be patient" or "If you love someone, you are patient with that person."

<u>kind</u>: or "If you love someone, you will be kind/good to that person." This kind of statement may be preferable for all the rest of verses 4-7.

conceited: "boastful" (RSV), "a braggart."

proud: this translates the verb "to puff up (with pride)" see 4.6, 18; 5.2; 8.1.

is not ill-mannered: "is not rude," "always behaves properly."

irritable: "easily provoked," "take offense quickly." The English idiom "to carry a chip on one's shoulder" well expresses the meaning, and other languages will have equivalent idioms of speech.

does not keep a record of wrongs: "does not cherish resentment." This phrase uses a verb which means "to add up," "to calculate," "to keep a record." The meaning may be stated: "If you love someone you do not keep on remembering the bad things he has done (to you)."

| 13.6-7 | TEV | RSV |
|---|---|---|
| | love is not happy with evil, but is happy with the truth. 7 Love never gives up; and its faith, hope, and patience never fail. | it does not rejoice at wrong, but rejoices in the right. 7 Love bears all things, believes all things, hopes all things, endures all things. |

In verse 6 one would expect Paul to oppose "good" to evil; instead he says truth (RSV "right"). The statement is not happy with evil means not to be happy when others do wrong, or go wrong, make mistakes; instead the person who loves rejoices when others do what is right or when right prevails. Here truth is not an abstract quality but right action, right behavior.

A comparison of TEV with RSV shows that the Greek text (as seen in RSV) has four verbs, with "all things" as the object of every verb. It would seem that the Greek pronoun "all" (here the plural neuter form) does not mean so much "everything" as "always." It is hard to understand "love believes all things"; this seems to say that the person who loves is gullible. So the meaning is, as TEV has it, its faith... never fail; or else, "never loses faith," "never stops believing." The object of faith (or, "to believe") here is uncertain: either God or else the eventual success of God's purposes in the world; "love never despairs."

The first verb (RSV "bears") is synonymous with the last verb (RSV "endures"). TEV takes the first one in a more general sense, including the affirmations of the next three verbs. The French common language translation has: "Love enables us to bear (or, endure) everything; it enables us in all circumstances to preserve our faith, our hope, and our patience."

| 13.8 | TEV | RSV |
|---|---|---|
| | Love is eternal. There are inspired messages, but they are temporary; there are gifts of speaking in strange tongues, but they will cease; there is knowledge, but it will pass. | Love never ends; as for prophecies, they will pass away; as for tongues, they will cease; as for knowledge, it will pass away. |

is eternal: the Greek is "never fails," which here means "never ends" (RSV), "never stops."

Paul compares love with three gifts from the Spirit: inspired messages (RSV "prophecies"): see verse 2; speaking in strange tongues: see 12.10; and knowledge: see 12.8; 13.2. All of these gifts are temporary and will soon disappear; but love endures.

13.9-10

| TEV | RSV |
|---|---|
| For our gifts of knowledge and of inspired messages are only partial; 10 but when what is perfect comes, then what is partial will disappear. | For our knowledge is imperfect and our prophecy is imperfect; 10 but when the perfect comes, the imperfect will pass away. |

In these verses Paul uses the two adjectives partial (RSV "imperfect") and perfect. The word "imperfect" may denote a moral flaw, which is not intended by the Greek phrase; rather "incomplete" or "limited." This contrasts with love, which is complete, whole. In English, perfect is the word most often used; the Greek word itself means mature, complete, whole.

13.11

| TEV | RSV |
|---|---|
| When I was a child, my speech, feelings, and thinking were all those of a child; now that I am a man, I have no more use for childish ways. | When I was a child, I spoke like a child, I thought like a child, I reasoned like a child; when I became a man, I gave up childish ways. |

Here Paul shows what he means about "the complete" doing away with "the incomplete": it is maturity displacing immaturity.

my speech, feelings, and thinking were all those of a child: or "I talked like a child, I reasoned like a child, I thought like a child." There is not much difference between the second and third verbs, which RSV translates "I thought...I reasoned." The second verb, in contrast with the third one, may perhaps denote basic outlook, attitude, while the third one indicates more the process of reasoning and thinking: "I had the outlook (or, attitude) of a child, I reasoned (or thought) like a child."

I have no more use for: "I am through with," "I have given up."

13.12

| TEV | RSV |
|---|---|
| What we see now is like a dim image in a mirror; then we shall see face-to-face. What I know now is only partial; then it will be complete—as complete as God's knowledge of me. | For now we see in a mirror dimly, but then face to face. Now I know in part; then I shall understand fully, even as I have been fully understood. |

we: this is inclusive; it means all Christians.

a dim image in a mirror: in those days mirrors were of polished metal (bronze or silver) and so gave an imperfect, distorted reflection. Paul compares that imperfect reflection with the perfect face-to-face vision. He is talking about the vision of God, of divine, eternal reality, which is now perceived in an imperfect way. For dim image the translation could be "an imperfect reflection," "a confusing reflection."

then: the reference (as in verse 10) is to the end, that is, the coming of Christ at the end of the age.

| 13.13 | TEV | RSV |
|---|---|---|
| | Meanwhile these three remain: faith, hope, and love; and the greatest of these is love. | So faith, hope, love abide, these three; but the greatest of these is love. |

Meanwhile: or "In truth," "As a fact," "As things are"—the same meaning that the Greek word has in 12.18.

remain: or "endure," "continue," "last."

# Chapter 14

More about Gifts from the Spirit: "More Instructions about Spiritual Gifts," "Speaking in Tongues."

Paul now concentrates his attention on the gift of speaking in strange tongues. He also writes about the gift of proclaiming God's message, especially in connection with order in the church worship service. Bare mention is made of some of the other gifts.

| 14.1 TEV | RSV |
|---|---|
| It is love, then, that you should strive for. Set your hearts on spiritual gifts, especially the gift of proclaiming God's message. | Make love your aim, and earnestly desire the spiritual gifts, especially that you may prophesy. |

The section begins with an order: "Strive for love," "Try to have love," "Put love first." And the next command, Set your hearts on spiritual gifts, has the same verb used in 12.31. Here Paul singles out the gift of proclaiming God's message as the one they should want more than any other (see 11.4).

| 14.2-3 TEV | RSV |
|---|---|
| The one who speaks in strange tongues does not speak to others but to God, because no one understands him. He is speaking secret truths by the power of the Spirit. 3 But the one who proclaims God's message speaks to people and gives them help, encouragement, and comfort. | For one who speaks in a tongue speaks not to men but to God; for no one understands him, but he utters mysteries in the Spirit. 3 On the other hand, he who prophesies speaks to men for their upbuilding and encouragement and consolation. |

Paul shows the difference between the two gifts of speaking in strange tongues and of proclaiming God's message. In the former case the person is speaking secret truths by the power of the Spirit. Here secret truths translates the same word translated secrets in 13.2. Here it could mean quite simply "unintelligible things," "unknown things." Paul's criticism of speaking in strange tongues is that it doesn't benefit others. Verse 2 can be translated "No one understands the person who speaks in strange tongues. By the power of God's Spirit that person says things that are unintelligible. He speaks only to God, not to other people."

by the power of the Spirit: literally "in spirit." It is assumed that the Greek phrase refers to the Spirit of God, and that is how it is translated by the majority of translations.

But the person who proclaims God's message uses language that is understood by others, and so what that person says helps other people.

<u>gives them help, encouragement, and comfort</u>: "he (or, what he says)
helps them, encourages them, and comforts them."

14.4    TEV          RSV
The one who speaks in strange   He who speaks in a tongue edifies
tongues helps only himself, but  himself, but he who prophesies
the one who proclaims God's mes- edifies the church.
sage helps the whole church.

<u>helps</u>: here, as in verse 3 (<u>gives them help</u>), this translates the
Greek verb "to build up" (RSV "edifies"): "helps people grow spiritually," "helps people develop their Christian faith." The one gift benefits only the individual who has it; the other gift benefits <u>the whole</u>
<u>church</u>.

14.5    TEV          RSV
 I would like for all of you  Now I want you all to speak in
to speak in strange tongues; but tongues, but even more to proph-
I would rather that you had the esy. He who prophesies is greater
gift of proclaiming God's message. than he who speaks in tongues,
For the person who proclaims God's unless some one interprets, so
message is of greater value than that the church may be edified.
the one who speaks in strange
tongues—unless there is someone
present who can explain what he
says, so that the whole church
may be helped.

Paul says quite clearly that he wishes all his readers had the
gift of speaking in strange tongues; but he prefers that they all had
<u>the gift of proclaiming God's message</u> (as in verse 1). Speaking in
strange tongues will help the whole church only if <u>there is someone</u>
<u>present who can explain what he says</u>. The ability to explain, or inter-
pret, is itself a gift from the Spirit (12.10,30).

14.6    TEV          RSV
So when I come to you, my brothers,  Now, brethren, if I come to
what use will I be to you if I you speaking in tongues, how shall
speak in strange tongues? Not a I benefit you unless I bring you
bit, unless I bring you some rev- some revelation or knowledge or
elation from God or some knowledge prophecy or teaching?
or some inspired message or some
teaching.

TEV has divided into two the rather long, complex sentence of this
verse, which is a rhetorical question, "how shall I benefit you...?"
(RSV), with the implied answer "In no way."
 <u>my brothers</u>: see 1.10.

14.6

Paul is saying that anything he might say in speaking in strange tongues would be of value to his listeners only if he (or someone else) were to interpret and so provide them with some revelation from God, and so forth. Speaking in strange tongues without interpretation is useless.

Paul lists four things: (1) revelation from God: "a truth revealed by God"; knowledge: as in 12.8; (3) inspired message: see 11.4; (4) teaching: see teachers in 12.28.

| 14.7-8       TEV | RSV |
|---|---|
| Take such lifeless musical instruments as the flute or the harp—how will anyone know the tune that is being played unless the notes are sounded distinctly? 8 And if the man who plays the bugle does not sound a clear call, who will prepare for battle? | If even lifeless instruments, such as the flute or the harp, do not give distinct notes, how will any one know what is played? 8 And if the bugle gives an indistinct sound, who will get ready for battle? |

Paul illustrates his point by speaking of musical instruments.

Take: this is used in the sense of "Consider," "Think of," "Take as an example."

the notes are sounded distinctly: "the notes are clearly played." Since the flute is a wind instrument and the harp is a string instrument, in some languages two different verbs may have to be used, one for each instrument: "to blow" and "to strum" (or something equivalent).

The second part of verse 7 may be restructured as a statement: "If the notes are not clearly played, no one will recognize the tune that is being played."

The bugle was the instrument used in battle to give instructions to the soldiers; different tunes meant different things (attack, retreat; gather, disperse; etc.), and so the bugler had to play the call clearly. Verse 8 may be presented as a statement: "If the man who plays the bugle does not sound a clear call, no one will prepare for battle," or "No one will get ready for battle if the bugle call is not clear."

| 14.9       TEV | RSV |
|---|---|
| In the same way, how will anyone understand what you are talking about if your message given in strange tongues is not clear? Your words will vanish in the air! | So with yourselves; if you in a tongue utter speech that is not intelligible, how will any one know what is said? For you will be speaking into the air. |

Paul makes the application to the situation in the Corinthian church.

you: this is plural.

The verse can be restructured as a statement: "In the same way, no one will understand what you are talking about if your message given in strange tongues is not made clear (or, explained)."

   Your words will vanish in the air!: this translates "you will be
speaking into the air" (RSV). There are other ways of saying this: "You
might as well be talking in an empty room," "It will be the same as
though you were talking to the walls," "You will be talking to the
wind."

14.10-11          TEV                              RSV
There are many different languages      There are doubtless many different
in the world, yet none of them is       languages in the world, and none
without meaning. 11 But if I do         is without meaning; 11 but if I
not know the language being spoken,     do not know the meaning of the
the person who uses it will be a        language, I shall be a foreigner to
foreigner to me and I will be a         the speaker and the speaker a
foreigner to him.                       foreigner to me.

   Now Paul uses foreign languages as an illustration.
   many different languages: little did Paul suspect how many! The
word here translated languages is not "tongues" but literally "voices"
or "sounds." Paul does not identify speaking in strange tongues as a
foreign language.
   yet none of them is without meaning: or "and all of them have
meaning."
   a foreigner: this translates a Greek word which is the source of
the word "barbarian," by which is meant (in Greek) "non-Greek." Unless
the language being spoken is understood by both the speaker and the
listener, they are both foreigners to each other.

14.12          TEV                                RSV
Since you are eager to have the         So with yourselves; since you are
gifts of the Spirit, you must try       eager for manifestations of the
above everything else to make           Spirit, strive to excel in build-
greater use of those which help         ing up the church.
to build up the church.

   The sentence in this verse can be divided into two: "You are, I
know, eager to have the gifts from the Spirit. So you must try above
everything else...."
   the gifts of the Spirit: this translates the Greek "the spirits";
RSV "manifestations of the Spirit"; here the word gifts seems better.
   to make greater use of those: or "to have more of the gifts."
   build up: as in verses 3-4.

14.13-14          TEV                             RSV
   The person who speaks in              Therefore, he who speaks in a
strange tongues, then, must pray        tongue should pray for the power
for the gift to explain what he         to interpret. 14 For if I pray in
says. 14 For if I pray in this          a tongue, my spirit prays but my
way, my spirit prays indeed, but        mind is unfruitful.
my mind has no part in it.

the gift to explain: as in 12.10.
Again Paul emphasizes that without the gift of interpretation, the gift of speaking in strange tongues is worthless.

in this way: that is, "in strange tongues." Paul is talking about praying in the church worship; and when praying in tongues, Paul says his spirit prays—that is, his inner being; but his mind, his thinking, his intelligence, is not involved. It is a purely emotional or ecstatic experience without rational content. Here "to pray in a tongue" is the same as "to pray in spirit."

| 14.15 | TEV | RSV |
|---|---|---|
| | What should I do, then? I will pray with my spirit, but I will pray also with my mind; I will sing with my spirit, but I will sing also with my mind. | What am I to do? I will pray with the spirit and I will pray with the mind also; I will sing with the spirit and I will sing with the mind also. |

Here Paul speaks of praying with my spirit in the same way as he does of praying with my mind; that is, both of them are things he can himself decide to do. So the translation may state "When I pray with my spirit, I will also pray with my mind." In both instances, in prayer and in singing (in church worship), Paul will use clear intelligible words besides the unintelligible sounds he makes while praying and singing in strange tongues.

| 14.16 | TEV | RSV |
|---|---|---|
| | When you give thanks to God in spirit only, how can an ordinary person taking part in the meeting say "Amen" to your prayer of thanksgiving? He has no way of knowing what you are saying. | Otherwise, if you bless[w] with the spirit, how can any one in the position of an outsider[x] say the "Amen" to your thanksgiving when he does not know what you are saying? |

[w]That is, *give thanks to God*
[x]Or *him that is without gifts*

you: singular; Paul addresses any one person in the congregation.
give thanks to God: the RSV footnote gives the meaning of "to bless" here (see 10.16).

an ordinary person: this translates the Greek verbal phrase "the person occupying the place of a private person" (RSV "an outsider"). In general the Greek term means someone who is not instructed, a lay person, a nonprofessional; in this context it would seem to mean someone, a Christian, that is (since in verses 23-24 this same word is used distinctly from the word for the unbeliever), who does not have the gift of the Spirit as does the one who is praying in spirit. Other translations of this phrase are "the simple Christian"; "the uninstructed"; "the ordinary person"; "the plain person"; "a simple listener in the congregation."

Amen: this is a Hebrew word meaning "So be it" or "It is so," used at the end of prayers.

The verse may be restructured as follows: "When you give thanks to God in spirit only, the ordinary (or, simple) person taking part in the meeting will not understand what you say. So how can he say 'Amen' when you finish your prayer?" Or "...what you say. So he cannot say 'Amen' to your prayer."

| 14.17 TEV | RSV |
|---|---|
| Even if your prayer of thanks to God is quite good, the other person is not helped at all. | For you may give thanks well enough, but the other man is not edified. |

Even if your prayer...is quite good: "Even though you have prayed well," "Even though the prayer you offer is appropriate."

the other person is not helped at all: or "no one else (beside yourself) is helped in the least." Here again the verb "to build up" is used (see verses 4-5). And here the other person is a general term for anyone else, not a particular term for a specific person.

| 14.18-19 TEV | RSV |
|---|---|
| I thank God that I speak in strange tongues much more than any of you. 19 But in church worship I would rather speak five words that can be understood, in order to teach others, than speak thousands of words in strange tongues. | I thank God that I speak in tongues more than you all; 19 nevertheless, in church I would rather speak five words with my mind, in order to instruct others, than ten thousand words in a tongue. |

Paul makes the claim in verse 18 only in order to show the small importance he attaches to his gift of speaking in strange tongues. Paul's point here, as throughout, is that the gift of speaking in tongues is of little, if any, value in church worship services.

much more: it should be noticed that this modifies I speak and not strange tongues. Paul does not say "I speak in more strange tongues than any of you" but "I speak more frequently in strange tongues than you do."

in church worship: this translates "in church" (RSV); but the translation should make it clear that the word designates the congregation itself or the worship service, and not a building called "church."

speak five words that can be understood: this translates "speak five words with my mind," by which is meant intelligible speech (as in verses 14-15).

| 14.20 TEV | RSV |
|---|---|
| Do not be like children in your thinking, my brothers; be children so far as evil is concerned, but be grown up in your thinking. | Brethren, do not be children in your thinking; be babes in evil, but in thinking be mature. |

like children: TEV uses a simile for the metaphor "children" (see RSV).

in your thinking: the Greek noun here is related to the verb used in 13.11 (translated feelings by TEV). Here "outlook" or "attitude" could serve as a translation.

be children so far as evil is concerned: here "children" is a figure for lack of experience, lack of knowledge; "be as innocent as children."

grown up: "mature"; the Greek word is the same as the one translated perfect in 13.10.


| 14.21 TEV | RSV |
|---|---|
| In the Scriptures it is written,<br>    "By means of men speaking<br>        strange languages<br>    I will speak to my people,<br>        says the Lord.<br>    I will speak through lips of<br>        foreigners,<br>        but even then my people<br>            will not listen to me." | In the law it is written, "By men<br>of strange tongues and by the<br>lips of foreigners will I speak<br>to this people, and even then<br>they will not listen to me, says<br>the Lord." |

the Scriptures: this translates the Greek word "law," by which is usually meant the Law of Moses, the Torah (see 9.8-9). The quotation that follows is from Isaiah 28.11-12.

men speaking strange languages: or "men speaking foreign languages." As RSV shows, there are two synonymous phrases used together: "by means of foreign languages" and "by means of the lips of foreigners." TEV has separated the two, placing one in line 1 and the other in line 3 for a more pleasing balance.

In languages where a poetic construction is not effective, the whole quotation may say in prose, "In the Scriptures it is written that the Lord (God) said, 'I will speak to my people through (or, by means of) foreigners speaking foreign languages, but even then my people will not listen to (or, obey) me.'" In the Old Testament passage the prophet is talking about the conquering Assyrians, through whom Yahweh will speak to his people Israel.


| 14.22 TEV | RSV |
|---|---|
| So then, the gift of speaking in strange tongues is proof for unbelievers, not for believers, while the gift of proclaiming God's message is proof for believers, not for unbelievers. | Thus, tongues are a sign not for believers but for unbelievers, while prophecy is not for unbelievers but for believers. |

This verse is strange; from what Paul has said so far, one would expect the exact opposite to be said here. Attempts have been made to extract from the Greek text a different meaning, but they are unconvincing.

proof: this translates the word "sign" (RSV), meaning here evidence of God's (or, the Spirit's) presence and power.

proclaiming God's message: see 11.4.

14.23          TEV

| | |
|---|---|
| If, then, the whole church meets together and everyone starts speaking in strange tongues—and if some ordinary people or unbelievers come in, won't they say that you are all crazy? | If, therefore, the whole church assembles and all speak in tongues, and outsiders or unbelievers enter, will they not say that you are mad? |

the whole church: "all the congregation," "all the believers."

some ordinary people: see verse 16.

The verse is composed of two conditional statements; the conclusion is stated as a rhetorical question. It may be preferable to restructure: "So when the whole congregation is meeting, if everyone starts speaking in strange tongues, then any ordinary people or unbelievers who come to the meeting will say that you are all crazy."

14.24-25          TEV

| | |
|---|---|
| But if everyone is proclaiming God's message when some unbeliever or ordinary person comes in, he will be convinced of his sin by what he hears. He will be judged by all he hears, 25 his secret thoughts will be brought into the open, and he will bow down and worship God, confessing, "Truly God is here among you!" | But if all prophesy, and an unbeliever or outsider enters, he is convicted by all, he is called to account by all, 25 the secrets of his heart are disclosed; and so, falling on his face, he will worship God and declare that God is really among you. |

proclaiming God's message: as in verse 22 and elsewhere in this chapter.

be convinced of his sin: "he will become aware of his sins."

by what he hears: this and by all he hears translate the Greek "by all," which may be understood as masculine, "by all people" (so RSV). It seems better, however, to understand it as TEV has: "by all that is said."

be judged: "he will realize that God judges," that is, that he is a sinner under God's judgment.

his secret thoughts will be brought into the open: this seems to imply public confession of sins.

Truly God is here among you!: "God is truly (or, really) present with you!" RSV has put this in indirect form, which may be preferable.

SECTION HEADING

Order in the Church: "Order in the Church's Worship Service."

In these verses (26-40) Paul concludes his treatment of the subject of the place and value of spiritual gifts in the worship of the church and emphasizes that all gifts should be employed in an orderly way, for the benefit of all.

| 14.26      TEV | RSV |
|---|---|
| This is what I mean, my brothers. When you meet for worship, one person has a hymn, another a teaching, another a revelation from God, another a message in strange tongues, and still another the explanation of what is said. Everything must be of help to the church. | What then, brethren? When you come together, each one has a hymn, a lesson, a revelation, a tongue, or an interpretation. Let all things be done for edification. |

This is what I mean: or "To conclude," "To sum up."
one person...another: TEV takes the Greek "each one" to be distributive, in the sense that the different elements of the worship (hymn, teaching, revelation, etc.) are distributed among the various people present. But RSV makes it appear that each person present had all five contributions to make to the service, which is not what Paul means.
a hymn: either an Old Testament psalm or a Christian composition.
a teaching...a revelation from God: see verse 6.
help to the church: the Greek says only "of help" (see verses 4-5), but it seems clear that here (as in verse 12) it is the whole congregation that is meant.

| 14.27-28      TEV | RSV |
|---|---|
| If someone is going to speak in strange tongues, two or three at the most should speak, one after the other, and someone else must explain what is being said. 28 But if no one is there who can explain, then the one who speaks in strange tongues must be quiet and speak only to himself and to God. | If any speak in a tongue, let there be only two or at most three, and each in turn; and let one interpret. 28 But if there is no one to interpret, let each of them keep silence in church and speak to himself and to God. |

Paul gives directions in these two verses on speaking in strange tongues in the worship service. The beginning of verse 27 may be translated: "If there are people present who want to speak in strange tongues...."
one after the other: that is, each one taking his turn instead of all of them speaking at the same time.
explain what is being said: that is, by someone who has the gift of interpretation (12.10).
speak only to himself and to God: that is, the person should not speak audibly at all, but rather whisper softly or else "speak" silently, as in the case of silent, private prayer.

14.29     TEV

Two or three who are given God's message should speak, while the others are to judge what they say.

14.29     RSV

Let two or three prophets speak, and let the others weigh what is said.

The prophets (see 12.28) are to exercise their gift in the same way; two or three of them should speak. Verse 29 does not explicitly say "one after the other" as in verse 27, but this is clearly implied (see verse 31). While they speak, the others are to pass judgment on them or on their message. Here the others are either other prophets or else those people who have the gift of distinguishing between genuine and false spiritual gifts (see 12.10). Not everyone who claimed to be speaking God's message was in fact led by the Spirit.

14.30-31     TEV

But if someone sitting in the meeting receives a message from God, the one who is speaking should stop. 31 All of you may proclaim God's message, one by one, so that everyone will learn and be encouraged.

14.30-31     RSV

If a revelation is made to another sitting by, let the first be silent. 31 For you can all prophesy one by one, so that all may learn and all be encouraged;

Order must be preserved whenever prophets are giving their inspired messages. Only one should speak at a time, for the benefit of the whole group.

learn: the inspired messages of the prophets would contain revelation of God's will for the people.

14.32-33a     TEV

The gift of proclaiming God's message should be under the speaker's control, 33 because God does not want us to be in disorder but in harmony and peace.

14.32-33a     RSV

and the spirits of prophets are subject to prophets. 33 For God is not a God of confusion but of peace.

In verse 32 RSV gives a literal translation of the Greek. The phrase "the spirits of the prophets" refers to their spiritual gifts (as in 12.10).

should be under the speaker's control: "must be controlled by the prophets themselves." The whole of verse 32 may be translated: "The prophets (or, Those who proclaim God's message) must be able to control their speaking."

God does not want us to be in...: or "God does not want disorder; he wants harmony and peace."

harmony and peace: TEV uses two words to translate one Greek word (RSV "peace"), and in some languages "peace" alone may be sufficient. In contrast with disorder (or, "confusion"), something like "harmony" or "order" may be preferable.

| 14.33b-34  TEV | RSV |
|---|---|
| As in all the churches of God's people, 34 the women should keep quiet in the meetings. They are not allowed to speak; as the Jewish Law says, they must not be in charge. | As in all the churches of the saints, 34 the women should keep silence in the churches. For they are not permitted to speak, but should be subordinate, as even the law says. |

In 11.5 Paul assumes that women will pray and proclaim God's message in public worship, so these verses contradict that assumption. Some believe that these verses were not written by Paul but inserted by a later copyist. In a few of the later Greek manuscripts, these verses come after verse 40; but they are not omitted by any Greek manuscript.

As in all the churches of God's people: most modern translations, like RSV and TEV, join this to what follows; older translations joined it to what precedes.

God's people: see 1.2,30.

in the meetings: this translates "in the churches" (see RSV), but the phrase means the public worship services of the church.

In defense of his instruction, Paul refers to the Jewish Law (or "the Law of Moses"). The injunction "they must be submissive" has as the implied object "to their husbands" (see the same verb in Col 3.18; Eph 5.21-22). Paul probably had Genesis 3.16 in mind; and see also 1 Corinthians 11.3. TEV has used the negative they must not be in charge; it might be better to say "they must be submissive" or "they must submit themselves to their husbands."

| 14.35  TEV | RSV |
|---|---|
| If they want to find out about something, they should ask their husbands at home. It is a disgraceful thing for a woman to speak in a church meeting. | If there is anything they desire to know, let them ask their husbands at home. For it is shameful for a woman to speak in church. |

If they want to find out about something: "If there is something they want to know," "If they have a question about anything."

a disgraceful thing: "a shameful thing," "an unbecoming thing."

| 14.36  TEV | RSV |
|---|---|
| Or could it be that the word of God came from you? Or are you the only ones to whom it came? | What! Did the word of God originate with you, or are you the only ones it has reached? |

With these two rhetorical questions Paul criticizes those who would want to disregard his instructions. He has appealed to what is done in the other churches (verse 33b), and here he reminds his critics that other churches have God's message.

the word of God: "the message from God."

The rhetorical questions may be phrased as statements: "The message from God did not come from you, and you are not the only ones who received it (or, to whom it went)."

| 14.37-38 TEV | RSV |
|---|---|
| If anyone supposes he is God's messenger or has a spiritual gift, he must realize that what I am writing to you is the Lord's command. 38 But if he does not pay attention to this, pay no attention to him. | If any one thinks that he is a prophet, or spiritual, he should acknowledge that what I am writing to you is a command of the Lord. 38 If any one does not recognize this, he is not recognized. |

God's messenger: this translates "a prophet" (see 11.4).

has a spiritual gift: "has received a gift from God's Spirit."

is the Lord's command: here Lord is Christ. Paul is saying that his instructions have the Lord's authority. He does not mean that he, Paul, is quoting what Christ had taught; rather he, Paul, as an apostle of Christ Jesus, is his authorized spokesman.

if he: "if someone (or, anyone)."

does not pay attention to this: "refuses to admit that this is so," that is, will not recognize that what Paul says has the Lord's authority behind it. The Greek verb "ignore" means to refuse to acknowledge the validity or truth of what is being said, or else to pay no attention to something.

pay no attention to him: this translates the Greek present passive of the same verb, "he is ignored," which TEV has taken as an implied imperative. But the passive voice may be a way of speaking about God, and so the meaning may be expressed, "God does not (or, will not) pay any attention to him."

Textual Note: many Greek manuscripts (including some of the oldest and the best) and ancient versions, instead of "he is ignored" (the present passive), have "let him ignore it" (the imperative third person singular). This would be a way of saying "If someone wants to ignore this, let him go on and do it—and bear the consequences!" Most modern translations follow the Greek text preferred by RSV and TEV.

| 14.39-40 TEV | RSV |
|---|---|
| So then, my brothers, set your heart on proclaiming God's message, but do not forbid the speaking in strange tongues. 40 Everything must be done in a proper and orderly way. | So, my brethren, earnestly desire to prophesy, and do not forbid speaking in tongues; 40 but all things should be done decently and in order. |

my brothers: see 1.10

set your heart on: see the same verb in 12.31; 14.1.

in a proper and orderly way: "properly and in order," "in a dignified and orderly manner."

# Chapter 15

The Resurrection of Christ: "Christ Has Been Raised from Death."
In this section (15.1-11) Paul talks about the resurrection and appearances of the risen Christ as the most important part of the gospel message. This truth was not only part of the gospel tradition that Paul had received; Paul himself had seen the risen Lord, and so he knew personally that Christ had been raised from death.

| 15.1-2 TEV | RSV |
|---|---|
| And now I want to remind you, my brothers, of the Good News which I preached to you, which you received, and on which your faith stands firm. 2 That is the gospel, the message that I preached to you. You are saved by the gospel if you hold firmly to it—unless it was for nothing that you believed. | Now I would remind you, brethren, in what terms I preached to you the gospel, which you received, in which you stand, 2 by which you are saved, if you hold it fast— unless you believed in vain. |

As the RSV text shows, verses 1-2 are one sentence in Greek; TEV has divided this sentence into two. RSV has transferred to verse 1 some elements of verse 2 ("in what terms") and has omitted from verse 2 the repetition "(which) I preached to you." The rearrangement has smoothed out what is a rather clumsy sentence in Greek.

I want to remind you: a polite way of bringing the matter to the attention of his readers. "I want you to remember."

the Good News: "the gospel message," "the message of salvation."

on which your faith stands firm: "in which you are spiritually secure." Paul compliments the Corinthian Christians for not having abandoned the Christian faith; they had remained loyal to the message he had proclaimed to them.

unless it was for nothing that you believed: "unless your faith was not genuine." The second part of verse 2 may be restructured as follows: "If you remain faithful to the gospel, you will be saved by it. But if your faith is not real, then you will not be saved."

| 15.3-5 TEV | RSV |
|---|---|
| I passed on to you what I received, which is of the greatest importance: that Christ died for our sins, as written in the Scriptures; 4 that he was buried and that he was raised to life three days later, as written in the Scriptures; 5 that he appeared to Peter and then to all twelve apostles. | For I delivered to you as of first importance what I also received, that Christ died for our sins in accordance with the scriptures, 4 that he was buried, that he was raised on the third day in accordance with the scriptures, 5 and that he appeared to Cephas, then to the twelve. |

I passed on...I received: see 11.2,23.

[ 142 ]

the greatest importance: the resurrection of Christ is the most important fact of the Christian faith.

died for our sins: "died so that our sins will be forgiven," "died so that God will forgive our sins."

as written in the Scriptures: there is no way of knowing what Old Testament passage Paul had in mind; perhaps Isaiah 53.4-12.

he was raised to life: "God raised him to life" or "God made him alive again." In terms of Paul's message, the translation should use the normal expression for being alive and not qualify it or modify it in any way.

three days later: the Greek phrase "on the third day" means "two days later."

as written in the Scriptures (verse 4): here it is even more uncertain what Old Testament passages Paul was referring to.

Peter: in Greek "Cephas" (as in 1.12). It seems better to use the more familiar name in translation, as TEV has done.

| 15.6-7 TEV | RSV |
|---|---|
| Then he appeared to more than five hundred of his followers at once, most of whom are still alive, although some have died. 7 Then he appeared to James, and afterward to all the apostles. | Then he appeared to more than five hundred brethren at one time, most of whom are still alive, though some have fallen asleep. 7 Then he appeared to James, then to all the apostles. |

his followers: this translates the Greek "brothers," but it seems reasonable to assume that they were not all male human beings. Or else, "more than five hundred believers."

at once: "at one time," "at the same time."

For the second part of verse 6 the following might be better: "Some of those people have already died, but most of them are still living."

James: most probably this is the brother of Jesus; he was a leader in the Jerusalem church (see Acts 12.17; Gal 1.19).

all the apostles: it is not clear what is the difference between this group and "the twelve" in verse 5. If there is a difference (which seems most likely), then here all the apostles includes others (such as Paul himself) besides the twelve disciples of Jesus.

| 15.8 TEV | RSV |
|---|---|
| Last of all he appeared also to me—even though I am like someone whose birth was abnormal.$^O$ | Last of all, as to one untimely born, he appeared also to me. |

$^O$whose birth was abnormal; or who was born at the wrong time.

he appeared also to me: at Paul's conversion on the road to Damascus (Acts 9.3-6).

I am like someone whose birth was abnormal: this translates what RSV translates as "one untimely born." The Greek word means an abortion,

[ 143 ]

a birth due to a miscarriage, a premature birth. Perhaps it was a term of abuse which Paul's opponents had applied to him—his conversion had not been a normal one; it was violent and unexpected. The TEV footnote gives another possible translation of the text.

| 15.9 | TEV | RSV |
|---|---|---|
| For I am the least of all the apostles—I do not even deserve to be called an apostle, because I persecuted God's church. | For I am the least of the apostles, unfit to be called an apostle, because I persecuted the church of God. |

the least of all the apostles: "I am the least important of all the apostles," "I am inferior to all other apostles," "all the other apostles are more important than me." Paul includes himself in the group; he too is an apostle (see 4.9).

The last part of the verse can be stated thus: "I persecuted the church of God, and so do not deserve to be called an apostle."

God's church: see 1.2.

| 15.10 | TEV | RSV |
|---|---|---|
| But by God's grace I am what I am, and the grace that he gave me was not without effect. On the contrary, I have worked harder than any of the other apostles, although it was not really my own doing, but God's grace working with me. | But by the grace of God I am what I am, and his grace toward me was not in vain. On the contrary, I worked harder than any of them, though it was not I, but the grace of God which is with me. |

by God's grace: "because of the grace of God," "by means of God's grace"; for grace see 1.4. Here the word denotes not only God's attitude (love) but also the expression of that love in blessing.

the grace that he gave me: here in the sense of blessings, of God's gifts to Paul.

was not without effect: "was not wasted," "was not worthless." In order to avoid the double negative the statement could be "and the grace that he gave me was effective."

God's grace working with me: this refers to the gifts from God that enabled Paul to do what he did as an apostle.

| 15.11 | TEV | RSV |
|---|---|---|
| So then, whether it came from me or from them, this is what we all preach, and this is what you believe. | Whether then it was I or they, so we preach and so you believed. |

whether it came from me or from them: "it makes no difference whether I preached the gospel to you or the other apostles did it." Paul says that the message that he proclaims is the same as that proclaimed by the other apostles. The verse may be restructured as follows: "All of us preach the same message. It makes no difference, then, whether I preached the gospel to you or the other apostles did it; we all preach the same message, the very message that you believe."

SECTION HEADING

Our Resurrection: "Christ's Resurrection and Our Resurrection." In this section (verses 12-34) Paul argues that Christ's resurrection and the resurrection of believers are closely related. If, as some were saying, believers are not resurrected, then Christ was not resurrected either, and so there is no gospel to proclaim. For the basic claim of the Christian message is that Christ was raised to life, and this means that believers in him will also be raised to life.

| 15.12 | TEV | RSV |
|---|---|---|
| | Now, since our message is that Christ has been raised from death, how can some of you say that the dead will not be raised to life? | Now if Christ is preached as raised from the dead, how can some of you say that there is no resurrection of the dead? |

our message: this is an inclusive pronoun; "the Christian message," "the message we proclaim."

Christ has been raised: or "God has raised Christ." It should be noticed that through this section (as in verse 4) the verb in Greek is in the perfect tense of the passive voice, "has been raised"; not simply "was raised" but "has been raised to life (and is still alive)." The passive is a way of saying that God raised Christ, as explicitly stated in verse 15 (the same verb "to raise" is used).

how can some of you say...?: this rhetorical question expresses surprise and censure: "you shouldn't say," "it is not true, as some of you say."

The verse may be restructured: "The Christian message is that God has raised Christ to life. So it is not true, as some of you are saying, that the dead will not be raised to life."

| 15.13-14 | TEV | RSV |
|---|---|---|
| | If that is true, it means that Christ was not raised; 14 and if Christ has not been raised from death, then we have nothing to preach and you have nothing to believe. | But if there is no resurrection of the dead, then Christ has not been raised; 14 if Christ has not been raised, then our preaching is in vain and your faith is in vain. |

If that is true: "If the dead are not raised to life," "If there is no resurrection (of the dead)."

it means: "then it follows"; "then we cannot say that Christ has been raised to life."

[ 145 ]

we have nothing to preach: we includes Paul and the other apostles; "we have no message to proclaim." RSV has "our preaching." The Greek noun means the message preached, not the act of preaching. "The message we preach is worth nothing (or, has no value)."

you have nothing to believe: "your faith is also worthless."

| 15.15 | TEV | RSV |
|---|---|---|
| More than that, we are shown to be lying about God, because we said that he raised Christ from death—but if it is true that the dead are not raised to life, then he did not raise Christ. | | We are even found to be misrepresenting God, because we testified of God that he raised Christ, whom he did not raise if it is true that the dead are not raised. |

Paul's logic is that the resurrection of the dead and the resurrection of Christ are like the two sides of a coin: they belong together, and to do away with one means to do away with the other. It is impossible to affirm that Christ was raised to life and at the same time say that the dead will not be raised. The verse may be translated as follows: "And it means also that we have been lying about God when we said that he raised Christ from death. For if the dead will not be raised to life, then God did not raise Christ."

| 15.16-17 | TEV | RSV |
|---|---|---|
| For if the dead are not raised, neither has Christ been raised. 17 And if Christ has not been raised, then your faith is a delusion and you are still lost in your sins. | | For if the dead are not raised, then Christ has not been raised. 17 If Christ has not been raised, your faith is futile and you are still in your sins. |

Paul again states that the two events are vitally connected; to deny one means to deny the other.

your faith is a delusion: the word translated delusion is synonymous with the word translated nothing in verse 14; "what you believe is false," "your faith in Christ is not real," "your faith in Christ does you no good."

you are still lost in your sins: "your sins have not been forgiven," "your lives are still ruled by sin."

| 15.18 | TEV | RSV |
|---|---|---|
| It would also mean that the believers in Christ who have died are lost. | | Then those also who have fallen asleep in Christ have perished. |

A further consequence of the denial of Christ's resurrection is that fellow believers who have died are not saved but lost.

have died: this translates the Greek "have fallen asleep," a common way of speaking about dying.

are lost: "have perished" (RSV).

15.19   TEV

If our hope in Christ is good for
this life only and no more,P then
we deserve more pity than anyone
else in all the world.

P If our hope in Christ is good
 for this life only and no more;
 *or* If all we have in this life
 is our hope in Christ.

      RSV

If for this life only we have
hoped in Christ, we are of all
men most to be pitied.

As the TEV text and footnote show, there are two ways of understanding the Greek text of the first part of this verse: (1) "only" modifies
"this life," as in RSV and TEV texts; (2) "only" modifies "our hope,"
as in the TEV footnote. Most modern translations understand the Greek
text as do the RSV and TEV texts.

 is good for this life only and no more: "has to do only with this
life, not the next one." "If the hope that Christ has given us applies
only to this life...."

 we deserve more pity than anyone else: "we are the most miserable
people in the world." This would be our condition if we did not believe
in the resurrection of Christ and our own resurrection.

15.20   TEV

 But the truth is that Christ
has been raised from death, as
the guarantee that those who sleep
in death will also be raised.

      RSV

 But in fact Christ has been
raised from the dead, the first
fruits of those who have fallen
asleep.

 But the truth is: "As a matter of fact."

 as the guarantee: "and this guarantees." The Greek word translated
"first fruits" by RSV refers to the first ripened heads of grain, which
indicated that the rest of the harvest would soon be ripe. The modern
equivalent would be "first installment," which implies that there is
more to come. To translate literally "the first fruits of those who
have fallen asleep" (RSV) is meaningless in English.

 those who sleep in death: "those who have died" (see verse 18). It
should be clear that Paul does not speak in this chapter of the resurrection of all the dead, but only of dead Christians, who are in union
with Christ (verse 22), those who belong to Christ (verse 23). Paul is
not talking here about the resurrection of all people but only of believers.

15.21-22   TEV

For just as death came by means of
a man, in the same way the rising
from death comes by means of a
man. 22 For just as all people die
because of their union with Adam,
in the same way all will be raised
to life because of their union with
Christ.

      RSV

For as by a man came death, by a
man has come also the resurrection
of the dead. 22 For as in Adam all
die, so also in Christ shall all
be made alive.

[ 147 ]

Paul argues for the resurrection of believers by drawing a parallel
between Adam as the head of a mortal race and Christ as the head of a
new humanity that, like him, will be raised from death.

death came: "death came to all people," "all people became mortal."
The translation should not make it appear that everyone died at the
same time.

by means of a man: "because of a man," "because of what a man did."

their union with Adam: this translates the phrase "in Adam," which
indicates the relation of every human being to Adam, the progenitor of
the human race; all are descended from him, and his sin and death means
that all people are mortal.

their union with Christ: this union is not a natural one, as is the
one to Adam; this union exists by means of faith.

| 15.23 TEV | RSV |
|---|---|
| But each one will be raised in his proper order: Christ, first of all; then, at the time of his coming, those who belong to him. | But each in his own order: Christ the first fruits, then at his coming those who belong to Christ. |

in his proper order: "in the right order." There is a progression
of events. Christ himself was the first to be raised; here the word in
Greek is the same "first fruits" of verse 20. A translation may want
to bring out the additional component of meaning: "Christ was raised
first, the guarantee that all will be raised."

his coming: when Christ returns at the end of the age.

those who belong to him: "his followers," "those who believe in
him." It may be preferable to say quite explicitly "Then, when Christ
comes, those who belong to him will be raised also."

| 15.24 TEV | RSV |
|---|---|
| Then the end will come; Christ will overcome all spiritual rulers, authorities, and powers, and will hand over the Kingdom to God the Father. | Then comes the end, when he delivers the kingdom to God the Father after destroying every ruler and every authority and power. |

the end: "the end of the age (or, the world)."

overcome: "destroy," "defeat."

spiritual rulers, authorities, and powers: these were thought of as
angels or (evil) spirits who control the universe.

hand over the Kingdom: or "hand over his kingly power," "transfer
his royal authority." The concept is that of the triumphant Christ
transferring his kingdom to God the Father. Here Kingdom can be thought
of as a realm or as kingly power.

| 15.25 TEV | RSV |
|---|---|
| For Christ must rule until God defeats all enemies and puts them under his feet. | For he must reign until he has put all his enemies under his feet. |

Here Paul makes use of the language of Psalm 110.1. The text says only "he must reign until he puts all enemies under his feet." As verses 27-28 make clear, the picture is that of God placing the enemies under Christ's feet, in accordance with the Christian interpretation of Psalm 110.1. So TEV makes explicit the various ones involved. The picture of enemies under the victor's feet is that of triumphant victory and shameful, public defeat. In some instances victorious kings would place their foot on the necks of their prostrate defeated enemies as a public sign of victory.

| 15.26 TEV | RSV |
|---|---|
| The last enemy to be defeated will be death. | The last enemy to be destroyed is death. |

Paul speaks of death as an enemy; and this enemy is defeated by Christ's resurrection. Or else Paul could be thinking specifically of the devil as the one who has the power of death, and the devil's defeat by Christ at the end of the age.

| 15.27 TEV | RSV |
|---|---|
| For the scripture says, "God put *all* things under his feet." It is clear, of course, that the words "all things" do not include God himself, who puts all things under Christ. | "For God[z] has put all things in subjection under his feet." But when it says, "All things are put in subjection under him," it is plain that he is excepted who put all things under him. |

[z]Greek *he*

RSV and TEV take the opening part of the verse as a quotation from Psalm 110.1, and TEV places *all* in italics because of its importance in the argument.
In the second part of the verse Paul makes the obvious comment that "all things" in Psalm 110.1 does not include God himself.

| 15.28 TEV | RSV |
|---|---|
| But when all things have been placed under Christ's rule, then he himself, the Son, will place himself under God, who placed all things under him; and God will rule completely over all. | When all things are subjected to him, then the Son himself will also be subjected to him who put all things under him, that God may be everything to every one. |

Here Paul repeats what he has said in verse 24: at the end Christ will abdicate his throne in favor of God, so to speak. Christ will hand all power over to God and subject himself to God.
God will rule completely over all: this translates what is literally "God will be all (things) in all (people)." In the context, it would seem that what is meant is God's complete and perfect power over

the whole universe and all mankind. But the idea "God will be everything to everyone" (as RSV has it) is also possible.

| 15.29 TEV | RSV |
|---|---|
| Now, what about those people who are baptized for the dead? What do they hope to accomplish? If it is true, as some claim, that the dead are not raised to life, why are those people being baptized for the dead? | Otherwise, what do people mean by being baptized on behalf of the dead? If the dead are not raised at all, why are people baptized on their behalf? |

In verses 29-34 Paul takes up the matter of baptism for the dead.
In this section he digresses somewhat from the main subject of the
resurrection of Christ and of believers.
people who are baptized for the dead: this is the only reference to
this practice and there is no further information about it. The language suggests that people were being baptized on behalf of people who
had already died without being baptized. Whether those dead people
were unbaptized believers or unbaptized unbelievers is impossible to
determine from the text. This kind of proxy baptism, so to speak, ap-
parently was thought to guarantee that the dead for whom living believers were being baptized would themselves be raised from death at
the end of the age.
Paul does not directly criticize the practice itself. What he does
say is that if there is no resurrection, proxy baptism is useless.
What do they hope to accomplish?: or "Why are they doing this?"
as some claim: TEV introduces this to make clear that this is what
some people in Corinth were saying (see verse 12).
The whole verse may be translated as follows: "There are those who
are baptized on behalf of dead people. Why should they do this if it
is true that the dead will not be raised to life?"

| 15.30 TEV | RSV |
|---|---|
| And as for us—why would we run the risk of danger every hour? | Why am I in peril every hour? |

us: here Paul refers to himself and his fellow apostles (see 4.9-
13). RSV takes the plural to be merely stylistic and interprets it to
mean that Paul is actually talking only about himself (as in the next
verse).

| 15.31 TEV | RSV |
|---|---|
| My brothers, I face death every day! The pride I have in you, in our life in union with Christ Jesus our Lord, makes me declare this. | I protest, brethren, by my pride in you which I have in Christ Jesus our Lord, I die every day! |

My brothers: see 1.10.

I face death every day: literally "I die every day" (RSV).

The text says: "I swear by my pride in you." Paul is proud of the Corinthian Christians, and his pride in them makes him affirm his own situation. The Greek phrase "by your boasting" could mean "by your pride in me," but most translations understand the text to mean what RSV and TEV have.

our life in union with Christ Jesus our Lord: our is inclusive, meaning Paul and his fellow believers in Corinth; and the whole phrase translates the Greek "in Christ Jesus our Lord" (see 1.2).

| 15.32 TEV | RSV |
|---|---|
| If I have, as it were, fought "wild beasts" here in Ephesus simply from human motives, what have I gained? But if the dead are not raised to life, then, as the saying goes, "Let us eat and drink, for tomorrow we will die." | What do I gain if, humanly speaking, I fought with beasts at Ephesus? If the dead are not raised, "Let us eat and drink, for tomorrow we die." |

as it were..."wild beasts": TEV adds as it were and the quotation marks to show that the words are not meant literally (see similar figure in 4.9).

from human motives: this translates the Greek phrase "according to man" (RSV "humanly speaking"). Others translate it "as the saying is," "as a mere mortal," "to use the popular expression." The phrase in Greek is enigmatic and it is impossible to be dogmatic about its meaning.

here in Ephesus: it is clear that Paul is writing from Ephesus (see 16.8).

what have I gained?: this is a rhetorical question, meaning "I have gained nothing."

The saying is from Isaiah 22.13. It might be phrased as follows: "We are going to die tomorrow, so we might as well eat and drink (all we want today)." But tomorrow is not intended as an exact prediction of the time of death, so it might be well to phrase it as follows: "We might as well eat and drink while we can, because we might die tomorrow." Underlying the exhortation is the belief that death is the end; all we have is this life on earth.

| 15.33-34 TEV | RSV |
|---|---|
| Do not be fooled. "Bad companions ruin good character." 34 Come back to your right senses and stop your sinful ways. I declare to your shame that some of you do not know God. | Do not be deceived: "Bad company ruins good morals." 34 Come to your right mind, and sin no more. For some have no knowledge of God. I say this to your shame. |

The quotation in verse 33 is a proverb attributed to the Greek poet Menander of the fourth century B.C.: "A person's character is ruined by bad companions." The "bad companions" here are the people in Corinth who deny the resurrection; the effect of this denial, Paul says, is seen in sinful behavior.

In verse 34 Paul urges his readers to change their thinking and their conduct.

do not know God: that is, don't have a vital relation with God.

SECTION HEADING

The Resurrection Body: "The Nature of the New Body after Death," "The Body Resurrected People Will Have."

Paul ends the chapter on resurrection by talking about the kind of body that resurrected believers will have. The discussion is prompted by the skeptical question as to what kind of body people will have who are raised from death. Greeks had no trouble with the concept of the immortal soul but could not admit a bodily resurrection.

| 15.35 TEV | RSV |
|---|---|
| Someone will ask, "How can the dead be raised to life? What kind of body will they have?" | But some one will ask, "How are the dead raised? With what kind of body do they come?" |

Someone will ask: this question would be a natural one; a living being requires a body, and it is clear that the physical body decays and disappears after death. RSV translates literally "With what kind of body do they come?" that is, come back to the world of the living.

| 15.36-37 TEV | RSV |
|---|---|
| You fool! When you plant a seed in the ground, it does not sprout to life unless it dies. 37 And what you plant is a bare seed, perhaps a grain of wheat or some other grain, not the full-bodied plant that will later grow up. | You foolish man! What you sow does not come to life unless it dies. 37 And what you sow is not the body which is to be, but a bare kernel, perhaps of wheat or of some other grain. |

Paul uses the analogy of the seed and the plant that springs to life from the seed.

unless it dies: Paul is stretching the language somewhat (as in John 12.24); here dies means (in terms of a seed) "decomposes." The seed disappears and the plant sprouts. If the seed remains intact, the plant does not grow. The statement in verse 36 may be translated: "A seed you plant in the ground has to die in order for the plant to sprout."

The obvious point Paul makes in verse 37 is that the plant that grows is radically different from the seed that was planted in the ground. The phrase "the body which is to be" (RSV) is represented in TEV by the full-bodied plant that will later grow up. It is not necessary to say "full-bodied" as TEV has done, and a satisfactory translation can be "the plant that will later grow."

| 15.38 | TEV | RSV |
|---|---|---|

God provides that seed with the body he wishes; he gives each seed its own proper body.

But God gives it a body as he has chosen, and to each kind of seed its own body.

Paul uses the word body as the plant which grows from the seed, since he is talking about the body of the resurrected person. He sees every plant as "the body" of the seed from which it sprang. The various kinds of plants are, for Paul's purpose here, different kinds of "bodies."

| 15.39 | TEV | RSV |
|---|---|---|

And the flesh of living beings is not all the same kind of flesh; human beings have one kind of flesh, animals another, birds another, and fish another.

For not all flesh is alike, but there is one kind for men, another for animals, another for birds, and another for fish.

Continuing his analogy, Paul says there are different kinds of flesh. This is not a scientific discussion of biology but a popular explanation of the matter. It would be wrong in this verse to translate "body" instead of flesh, as some translations do. Paul could easily have said "body" here if he had meant it; but he has chosen to speak of the material of which a living body is made, flesh.

| 15.40-41 | TEV | RSV |
|---|---|---|

And there are heavenly bodies and earthly bodies; the beauty that belongs to heavenly bodies is different from the beauty that belongs to earthly bodies. 41 The sun has its own beauty, the moon another beauty, and the stars a different beauty; and even among stars there are different kinds of beauty.

There are celestial bodies and there are terrestrial bodies; but the glory of the celestial is one, and the glory of the terrestrial is another. 41 There is one glory of the sun, and another glory of the moon, and another glory of the stars; for star differs from star in glory.

Here Paul appeals to the differences that exist between heavenly bodies and earthly bodies, and the differences among the various celestial bodies. By heavenly bodies Paul seems to be talking about the sun, moon, stars, and planets, not about the inhabitants of heaven (that is, the angels). But it is difficult to understand what is meant by earthly bodies in contrast to such heavenly bodies; they must be the bodies of living beings on earth.

beauty: or "splendor" or "glory."

In verse 41 "splendor" better fits the context than beauty: Paul is talking about the different degrees of brilliance which characterize the various celestial bodies.

| 15.42 TEV | RSV |
|---|---|
| This is how it will be when the dead are raised to life. When the body is buried, it is mortal; when raised, it will be immortal. | So is it with the resurrection of the dead. What is sown is perishable, what is raised is imperishable. |

This is how it will be: Paul alludes specifically to the difference between the bare seed that is planted and the plant that grows from it (verse 37). The body itself is mortal; the resurrected believer will be immortal, and so will the "body" he will have.

mortal...immortal: or else verbal phrases may be used: "a body that dies...a body that never dies."

In verses 42-44 Paul uses the passive voice of the verb "to plant" (or, "to sow," as in RSV). TEV has abandoned the figure and uses the verb "to bury." Other translations may choose to do the same, if the verb "to plant" here is liable to cause difficulty for the reader.

| 15.43-44 TEV | RSV |
|---|---|
| When buried, it is ugly and weak; when raised, it will be beautiful and strong. 44 When buried, it is a physical body; when raised, it will be a spiritual body. There is, of course, a physical body, so there has to be a spiritual body. | It is sown in dishonor, it is raised in glory. It is sown in weakness, it is raised in power. 44 It is sown a physical body, it is raised a spiritual body. If there is a physical body, there is also a spiritual body. |

Paul uses three more contrastive pairs to show what kind of body the resurrected believer will have.

ugly...beautiful: this is what is meant by RSV "dishonor...glory"; or else something like "contemptible...glorious."

weak...strong: "powerless...powerful."

physical...spiritual: this is the climax of Paul's argument. Throughout the whole section he has tried to show that each mode of existence, human and animal, earthly and heavenly, has its own and appropriate kind of body. Physical existence requires a physical body, and spiritual existence, after death, requires a spiritual body. And since the one (the physical body) exists, the other one is also bound to exist—for there is no existence without a body.

| 15.45 TEV | RSV |
|---|---|
| For the scripture says, "The first man, Adam, was created a living being"; but the last Adam is the life-giving Spirit. | Thus it is written, "The first man Adam became a living being"; the last Adam became a life-giving spirit. |

Paul quotes Genesis 2.7. Here he makes a play on words which neither RSV nor TEV is able to reproduce. In verse 44 Paul says "*psuchikon* body" (translated physical body) and "*pneumatikon* body" (translated spiritual body). Here in verse 45, citing the Greek translation of

Genesis 2.7, he says Adam was created "a living *psuche*" (translated a
living being); but the last Adam (Christ) is "a life-giving *pneuma*"
(translated the life-giving Spirit). Even though it may be impossible
to reproduce the word play in translation, the meaning is given accu-
rately in RSV and TEV.

the last Adam: the reference is to the risen Christ. It is better
not to say explicitly Jesus Christ; but if the lack of identification
makes the text difficult for the reader, it may be necessary to say,
"the last Adam, that is, (the risen) Christ."

is the life-giving Spirit: or "has become the life-giving Spirit,"
"the Spirit who gives eternal life (to us)."

15.46-47          TEV                              RSV
It is not the spiritual that comes    But it is not the spiritual which
first, but the physical, and then     is first but the physical, and
the spiritual. 47 The first Adam,     then the spiritual. 47 The first
made of earth, came from the earth;   man was from the earth, a man of
the second Adam came from heaven.     dust; the second man is from
                                      heaven.

Paul uses the same two adjectives used in verse 44: spiritual...
physical. It may be necessary to say "the spiritual being (or, the
spiritual man)...the physical being (or, the physical man)."

made of earth: this translates an adjective in Greek which RSV
renders "a man of dust." This Greek adjective is related to the word
used in the Greek translation of Genesis 2.7, meaning "dirt, soil."
This expression emphasizes the mortality of human beings.

15.48-49          TEV                              RSV
Those who belong to the earth are     As was the man of dust, so are
like the one who was made of earth;   those who are of the dust; and
those who are of heaven are like      as is the man of heaven, so are
the one who came from heaven.         those who are of heaven. 49 Just
49 Just as we wear the likeness       as we have borne the image of the
of the man made of earth, so we       man of dust, we shall*a* also bear
will wear*q* the likeness of the      the image of the man of heaven.
Man from heaven.

                                      *a*Other ancient authorities read
*q*we will wear; *some manuscripts*    *let us*
*have* let us wear.

In verse 48 Paul distinguishes between the two races: the natural
race of humankind (Those who belong to the earth) is like Adam: the
spiritual race (those who are of heaven) is like Christ.
In verse 49 Paul speaks of the destiny of believers (the we includes all believers): all believers are like Adam, as physical
beings; but the time will come (at the end) when believers will be
like Christ, the Man from heaven. TEV has wear the likeness of in an
attempt to give some of the connotation of the Greek verb "to wear
(clothes)."

[ 155 ]

Textual Note: as the RSV and TEV footnotes show, instead of the future indicative we will wear, many good Greek manuscripts and ancient versions have the subjunctive "let us wear." Most modern translations follow the text preferred by RSV and TEV.

| 15.50 TEV | RSV |
|---|---|
| What I mean, brothers, is that what is made of flesh and blood cannot share in God's Kingdom, and what is mortal cannot possess immortality. | I tell you this, brethren: flesh and blood cannot inherit the kingdom of God, nor does the perishable inherit the imperishable. |

brothers: see 1.10.
Paul's argument is that believers must undergo the change at death and resurrection from physical beings to spiritual beings, because physical beings, made of flesh and blood, cannot have a part in God's Kingdom, which is here eternal life with God after resurrection.
share...possess: these two translate the same Greek verb "inherit" (see RSV); "have a part in," "belong to" (see 6.9).

| 15.51-52 TEV | RSV |
|---|---|
| Listen to this secret truth: we shall not all die, but when the last trumpet sounds, we shall all be changed in an instant, as quickly as the blinking of an eye. For when the trumpet sounds, the dead will be raised, never to die again, and we shall all be changed. | Lo! I tell you a mystery. We shall not all sleep, but we shall all be changed, 52 in a moment, in the twinkling of an eye, at the last trumpet. For the trumpet will sound, and the dead will be raised imperishable, and we shall be changed. |

TEV rearranges the material in the sentence, which includes the two verses. RSV follows the order of the material in the Greek text.
secret truth: "mystery," "secret," "unknown fact."
die: this translates the Greek "sleep" (as in verse 18). What Paul means here is that we (this includes all believers) shall not all die before the end comes; some will still be alive at that time.
the last trumpet sounds: this is thought of as a trumpet blown by an angel to signal the end of the age. If possible it is better to say "when the trumpet is blown to signal the end of the age," without specifically indicating an angel as the one who will blow the trumpet (see other references to the trumpet at Matt 24.31; 1 Thes 4.16).
the dead will be raised, never to die again: "all those who have died will be raised (to life) and live forever." The Greek word translated never to die again is an adjective meaning "imperishable," "that does not decay" (as in verse 42, which has "perishable" and "imperishable").
we shall all be changed: here again Paul is referring to those who will still be living when the end comes; they will be transformed immediately from living mortal creatures to living immortal beings.

15.53          TEV

For what is mortal must be changed
into what is immortal; what will
die must be changed into what cannot die.

RSV

For this perishable nature must
put on the imperishable, and this
mortal nature must put on immortality.

Paul uses two synonymous pairs of contrasting antonyms: "perishable...imperishable; mortal...immortality." If two synonymous pairs
are difficult or strange, a translation may express the meaning with
just one contrasting pair: "mortal...immortal."

RSV "this perishable nature...this mortal nature" translates what
in Greek is "this perishable thing...this mortal thing." It might be
better to say "this perishable being...this mortal being." However it
is translated, it should be clear that Paul is talking about human
beings, who are mortal and subject to decay.

be changed into: this translates the verb "to clothe oneself with."
The figure of "to clothe" (see RSV) may carry the idea of a change in
outward appearance only, which is not what Paul meant. Here the "cloth-
ing" is, in fact, the spiritual body which the resurrected ones will
have.


15.54          TEV

So when this takes place, and the
mortal has been changed into the
immortal, then the scripture will
come true: "Death is destroyed;
victory is complete!"

RSV

When the perishable puts on the
imperishable, and the mortal puts
on immortality, then shall come
to pass the saying that is written:
      "Death is swallowed up in
            victory."

when this takes place and the mortal has been changed into the
immortal: this represents the repetition of "when this that is perishable clothes itself with what is imperishable, and this that is mortal
clothes itself with immortality."

the scripture: Paul quotes Isaiah 25.8 in a form different both
from the Hebrew text and from the ancient Greek translation, the Septuagint. The literal form of the quotation is "Death is swallowed up
in victory." Here "swallowed up" means "destroyed, done away with."
The translation can be "The victory is won, and death has been destroyed."


15.55          TEV

"Where, Death, is your victory?
Where, Death, is your power to
      hurt?"

RSV

"O death, where is thy vic-
      tory?
O death, where is thy sting?"

This verse is a quotation from Hosea 13.14 which agrees neither
with the Hebrew text nor with the Septuagint. The two rhetorical questions can be represented as declarations: "Death is no longer victorious! (or, Death has been defeated!) Death is no longer able to harm
us!"

15.55

power to hurt: this translates a Greek noun which may mean (1) "a goad," the sharp, pointed instrument used to guide and to punish animals, especially oxen; or (2) "a sting" of an insect (such as a scorpion) or of a snake, which may not only hurt but can kill. So if Paul has in mind the poisonous sting of an animal, the meaning is "Where, Death is your power to kill?"

| 15.56 | TEV | RSV |
|---|---|---|

Death gets its power to hurt from sin, and sin gets its power from the Law.

The sting of death is sin, and the power of sin is the law.

This verse is a parenthetical comment; the thought goes directly from verse 55 to verse 57.

Death gets its power to hurt from sin: this translates "The sting of death is sin." Paul's statement is that death is harmful and fearful because it is the result of sin (so Gen 3).

sin gets its power from the Law: by this Paul means that it is the (Jewish) Law which makes sin a threat, since the Law provides punishment for those who sin.

| 15.57 | TEV | RSV |
|---|---|---|

But thanks be to God who gives us the victory through our Lord Jesus Christ!

But thanks be to God, who gives us the victory through our Lord Jesus Christ.

thanks be to God: "let us all thank God," "we must all praise God."

through our Lord Jesus Christ: "because of what our Lord Jesus Christ has done." Or the whole statement can be, "Our Lord Jesus Christ makes it possible for us to have the victory (over death) which God gives us. Let us thank God for that!"

| 15.58 | TEV | RSV |
|---|---|---|

So then, my dear brothers, stand firm and steady. Keep busy always in your work for the Lord, since you know that nothing you do in the Lord's service is ever useless.

Therefore, my beloved brethren, be steadfast, immovable, always abounding in the work of the Lord, knowing that in the Lord your labor is not in vain.

stand firm and steady: "continue to be faithful and (spiritually) strong."

the Lord: this refers to Jesus Christ.

The elements in the last sentence may be reversed as follows: "You know that everything you do in the Lord's service is worthwhile (or, of value), so keep busy working for him."

# Chapter 16

SECTION HEADING

The Offering for Fellow Believers: "The Offering for the Believers in Jerusalem."
In this section (verses 1-4) Paul talks about the money he is raising among Christians in his travels, to help the needy Christians in Jerusalem.

16.1          TEV
Now, concerning what you wrote about the money to be raised to help God's people in Judea. You must do what I told the churches in Galatia to do.

RSV
Now concerning the contribution for the saints: as I directed the churches of Galatia, so you also are to do.

concerning what you wrote: see 7.1.
God's people: see 1.2.
in Judea: TEV includes this in order to be more specific (for further references to this offering see 2 Cor 8.1-4; 9.1-5; Rom 15.25-28; see also Acts 11.29-30). If a translation wants to be specific it may say "God's people (or, our fellow believers) in Jerusalem" (as in verse 3).
Galatia: a Roman province in what is now Turkey.

16.2          TEV
Every Sunday each of you must put aside some money, in proportion to what he has earned, and save it up, so that there will be no need to collect money when I come.

RSV
On the first day of every week, each of you is to put something aside and store it up, as he may prosper, so that contributions need not be made when I come.

Sunday: literally "the first day of the week." This may refer to the time when Christians would gather for worship.
in proportion to what he has earned: "in proportion to his gains." Paul is asking each one to give an amount proportionate to what that person has earned. The verse may be broken in two sentences, with a full stop after save it up. The next sentence could be "If you do this, then there will be no need...."
collect money: "take up offerings."

16.3          TEV
After I come, I shall give letters of introduction to the men you have approved, and send them to take your gift to Jerusalem.

RSV
And when I arrive, I will send those whom you accredit by letter to carry your gift to Jerusalem.

16.3

A comparison of RSV with TEV shows that TEV takes the letters of introduction to be from Paul, while RSV takes them to be from the believers in Corinth. Either interpretation of the text is defensible; most modern translations understand the text as TEV has it.

| 16.4 TEV | RSV |
|---|---|
| If it seems worthwhile for me to go, then they can go along with me. | If it seems advisable that I should go also, they will accompany me. |

worthwhile: "right," "sensible."


SECTION HEADING

Paul's Plans: "Paul's Future Travels."
In this section (verses 5-12) Paul gives information on what he plans to do.

| 16.5 TEV | RSV |
|---|---|
| I shall come to you after I have gone through Macedonia—for I have to go through Macedonia. | I will visit you after passing through Macedonia, for I intend to pass through Macedonia, |

come to you: "go to you," "visit you" (RSV).
Macedonia: a Roman province corresponding to what is now northern Greece; its capital was Thessalonica. A translator should consult a map to see how Paul would go from Ephesus to Corinth via Macedonia.
I have to go: "I plan to go," "I will be going."


| 16.6 TEV | RSV |
|---|---|
| I shall probably spend some time with you, perhaps the whole winter, and then you can help me to continue my trip, wherever it is I shall go next. | and perhaps I will stay with you or even spend the winter, so that you may speed me on my journey, wherever I go. |

winter: Corinth was a seaport; where Paul planned to go next he does not say. Navigation on the seas stopped in the winter (see Acts 27.9,12).
you can help me: that is, by contributing the money he would need for his travel expenses.


| 16.7 TEV | RSV |
|---|---|
| I want to see you more than just briefly in passing; I hope to spend quite a long time with you, if the Lord allows. | For I do not want to see you now just in passing; I hope to spend some time with you, if the Lord permits. |

The first part of this verse may be translated "I do not want just a short visit with you...."

the Lord: either God or Jesus Christ; probably the latter.

16.8-9      TEV                       RSV

I will stay here in Ephesus until the day of Pentecost. 9 There is a real opportunity here for great and worthwhile work, even though there are many opponents. | But I will stay in Ephesus until Pentecost, 9 for a wide door for effective work has opened to me, and there are many adversaries.

Ephesus: the capital of the Roman province of Achaia (see verse 15).

Pentecost: the Jewish festival of wheat harvest on the sixth day of the month of Sivan (around May 20). The name "Pentecost" (meaning "fiftieth") comes from the fact that the festival was held fifty days after Passover.

real opportunity: literally "a wide door is open."

The first part of verse 9 may be translated "I have a great opportunity to do Christian work that will produce good results."

16.10      TEV                       RSV

If Timothy comes your way, be sure to make him feel welcome among you, because he is working for the Lord, just as I am. | When Timothy comes, see that you put him at ease among you, for he is doing the work of the Lord, as I am.

If Timothy comes your way: "When Timothy gets there (or, arrives)"; see 4.17

16.11      TEV                       RSV

No one should look down on him, but you must help him continue his trip in peace, so that he will come back to me; for I am expecting him back with the brothers. | So let no one despise him. Speed him on his way in peace, that he may return to me; for I am expecting him with the brethren.

look down on him: "treat him with disrespect."

the brothers: it is not certain who these are; perhaps with Timothy (see 4.17) Paul is sending other Christian workers to take this letter to Corinth.

16.12      TEV                       RSV

Now, about brother Apollos. I have often encouraged him to visit you with the other brothers, but he is not completely convinced[n] | As for our brother Apollos, I strongly urged him to visit you with the other brethren, but it was not at all his will[b] to come

| | |
|---|---|
| that he should go at this time. When he gets the chance, however, he will go. | now. He will come when he has opportunity. |

*b*Or *God's will for him*

*r*he is not completely convinced; *or* it is not at all God's will.

Now, about: this is the same phrase in Greek as in 7.1; 8.1; 12.1; 16.1. As in the other instances, it may mean that the Corinthian Christians had written Paul about Apollos.

Apollos: see 1.12.

the other brothers: perhaps the same as the brothers in verse 11.

As RSV and TEV footnotes show, the Greek "(his) will" may refer to Apollos or to God.


SECTION HEADING

Final Words: "Last Instructions."


| 16.13-14 TEV | RSV |
|---|---|
| Be alert, stand firm in the faith, be brave, be strong. 14 Do all your work in love. | Be watchful, stand firm in your faith, be courageous, be strong. 14 Let all that you do be done in love. |

Be alert: this is spiritual alertness, a careful attention to the needs of the Christian community.


| 16.15-16 TEV | RSV |
|---|---|
| You know about Stephanas and his family; they are the first Christian converts in Achaia and have given themselves to the service of God's people. I beg you, my brothers, 16 to follow the leadership of such people as these, and of anyone else who works and serves with them. | Now, brethren, you know that the household of Stephanas were the first converts in Achaia, and they have devoted themselves to the service of the saints; 16 I urge you to be subject to such men and to every fellow worker and laborer. |

Stephanas and his family: see 1.16.

Achaia: a Roman province corresponding to what is now southern Greece; its capital city was Corinth.

my brothers: see 1.10

It should be noticed that I beg you, my brothers, at the end of verse 15, comes at the beginning of the verse in the Greek text; RSV places it at the beginning of verse 16.

follow the leadership of: "obey," "be submissive to." This is the same Greek verb that is used in 14.34.

16.17-18          TEV
    I am happy about the coming
of Stephanas, Fortunatus, and
Achaicus; they have made up for
your absence 18 and have cheered
me up, just as they cheered you
up. Such men as these deserve
notice.

          RSV
    I rejoice at the coming of Steph-
anas and Fortunatus and Achaicus,
because they have made up for your
absence; 18 for they refreshed my
spirit as well as yours. Give rec-
ognition to such men.

    Perhaps <u>Stephanas, Fortunatus, and Achaicus</u> brought the letter
from the Corinthian church to Paul (see 7.1).
    <u>just as they cheered you up</u>: it is not certain how these men had
cheered up the Corinthian Christians; perhaps it was by their willing-
ness to go and see Paul.
    <u>notice</u>: "to be highly regarded," "to be praised."


16.19-20          TEV
    The churches in the province
of Asia send you their greetings;
Aquila and Priscilla and the church
that meets in their house send warm
Christian greetings. 20 All the
brothers here send greetings.
    Greet one another with a
brotherly kiss.

          RSV
    The churches of Asia send
greetings. Aquila and Prisca, together with the church in their
house, send you hearty greetings
in the Lord. 20 All the brethren
send greetings. Greet one another
with a holy kiss.

    <u>Asia</u>: a Roman province in what is now Turkey; its capital city was
Ephesus.
    <u>Aquila and Priscilla</u>: a Christian couple, close friends and compan-
ions of Paul (see Acts 18.1-19).
    <u>a brotherly kiss</u>: "a Christian kiss." This greeting became a reg-
ular part of the worship service.


16.21          TEV
    With my own hand I write this:
*Greetings from Paul.*

          RSV
    I, Paul, write this greeting
with my own hand.

    <u>With my own hand</u>: now Paul writes; the rest of the letter he has
dictated. Perhaps Sosthenes (see 1.1) was the one to whom Paul dictated
the letter. The verse may be translated "I write this greeting myself.
*Paul*."


16.22          TEV
    Whoever does not love the
Lord—a curse on him!
    *Marana tha*—Our Lord, come!

          RSV
    If any one has no love for the
Lord, let him be accursed. Our
Lord, come!*c*

    *c*Greek *Maranatha*

the Lord: this refers to Jesus Christ.

a curse: "God's curse," "God's punishment." This is the same word used in 12.3. Perhaps Paul had some particular person or group in mind.

*Marana tha:* this is the transliteration of the Aramaic phrase which means "Our Lord, come!" TEV gives both the transliterated Aramaic phrase and its meaning in English. A translation may omit the transliterated Aramaic, as RSV does.

| 16.23-24 | TEV | RSV |
|---|---|---|
| | The grace of the Lord Jesus be with you. | The grace of the Lord Jesus be with you. 24 My love be with you all in Christ Jesus. Amen. |
| | 24 My love be with you all in Christ Jesus. | |

grace: see 1.4.

in Christ Jesus: "in union with Christ Jesus." The verse may be "I send my love to all of you who live in union with Christ Jesus." See 1.2.

Textual Note: RSV has "Amen" at the end; TEV, following the Greek New Testament of the United Bible Societies, omits the closing word. The evidence is divided, and a translation may choose to include the word. For its meaning see 14.16.

# Selected Bibliography

## Text

The Greek New Testament. Third edition 1975. K. Aland, M. Black, C. M.
    Martini, B. M. Metzger, and A. Wikgren, editors. Stuttgart:
    United Bible Societies.

## Lexicon

Arndt, William F., and F. Wilbur Gingrich. Second edition 1979. A Greek-
    English Lexicon of the New Testament and Other Early Christian
    Literature. Chicago: University of Chicago Press.

## Commentaries

Craig, Clarence Tucker. 1953. 1 Corinthians (Interpreter's Bible, volume
    X). New York: Abingdon-Cokesbury.

Findlay, G. G. n.d. 1 Corinthians (Expositor's Greek Testament). Grand
    Rapids, Michigan: Eerdmans.

Parry, R. St. John. 1937. 1 Corinthians (Cambridge Greek Testament).
    Cambridge: University Press.

Robertson, Archibald, and Alfred Plummer. 1911. 1 Corinthians (Interna-
    tional Critical Commentary). New York: Charles Scribner's Sons.

# Glossary

This glossary contains terms which are technical from an exegetical or a linguistic viewpoint. Other terms not defined here may be referred to in a Bible dictionary.

abstract refers to terms which designate the qualities and quantities (that is, the features) of objects and events but which are not objects or events themselves. For example, "red" is a quality of a number of objects but is not a thing in and of itself. Typical abstracts include "goodness," "beauty," "length," "breadth," and "time."

active. See voice.

adjective is a word which limits, describes, or qualifies a noun. In English, "red," "tall," "beautiful," and "important" are adjectives.

adverb is a word which limits, describes, or qualifies a verb, an adjective, or another adverb. In English, "quickly," "soon," "primarily," and "very" are adverbs.

adversative describes something opposed to or in contrast with something already stated. "But" and "however" are adversative conjunctions.

agent is that which accomplishes the action in a sentence or clause, regardless of whether the grammatical construction is active or passive. In "John struck Bill" (active) and "Bill was struck by John" (passive), the agent in either case is John.

analogy is a comparison between two items that have some features which are similar.

ancient versions. See versions.

antonym is a word which means the opposite of another word; for example, "good" is an antonym of "evil," and "big" is an antonym of "little."

Aramaic is a language that was widely used in Southwest Asia before the time of Christ. It became the common language of the Jewish people in Palestine in place of Hebrew, to which it is related.

clause is a grammatical construction, normally consisting of a subject and a predicate.

[ 167 ]

**common language translation** is one that uses only that portion of the total resources of a language that is understood and accepted by all as good usage. Excluded are features peculiar to a dialect, substandard or vulgar language, and technical or highly literary language not understood by all.

**conjunctions** are words which serve as connectors between words, phrases, clauses, and sentences. "And," "but," "if," and "because" are typical conjunctions in English.

**construction.** See **structure.**

**context** is that which precedes and/or follows any part of a discourse. For example, the context of a word or phrase in Scripture would be the other words and phrases associated with it in the sentence, paragraph, section, and even the entire book in which it occurs. The context of a term often affects its meaning, so that a word does not mean exactly the same thing in one context that it does in another.

**copyists** were people who made handwritten copies of books, before the invention of printing. See **manuscripts.**

**cultural equivalent** is a kind of translation in which certain details from the culture of the source language are changed because they have no meaning or may even carry a wrong meaning for speakers of the receptor language. Cultural equivalent translation should be used only when absolutely necessary for conveying the intended meaning, and it may be important to add an explanatory note. See **culture.**

**culture** is the sum total to the ways of living built up by the people living in a certain geographic area. A culture is passed on from one generation to another, but undergoes development or gradual change. See **cultural equivalent.**

**direct object** is the goal of an event or action specified by a verb. In "John hit the ball," the direct object of "hit" is "ball."

**discourse** is the connected and continuous communication of thought by means of language, whether spoken or written. The way in which the elements of a discourse are arranged is called **discourse structure.** **Direct discourse** is the reproduction of the actual words of one person quoted and included in the discourse of another person; for example, "He declared, '*I will have nothing to do with this man.*'" **Indirect discourse** is the reporting of the words of one person within the discourse of another person, but in an altered grammatical form rather than as an exact quotation; for example, "He said *he would have nothing to do with that man.*"

**distributive** refers not to the group as a whole, but to the members of the group. **Distributive singular** is a form that refers to each individual within the group.

double negative is a grammatical construction in which two negative words are used in the same clause. Usually two negatives produce a positive meaning ("He did not say nothing" means "He did say something"). In some languages, however, a double negative is an emphatic negative (as in Greek, where "not no" means *definitely* not").

emphasis (emphatic) is the special importance given to an element in a discourse, sometimes indicated by the choice of words or by position in the sentence. For example, in "Never will I eat pork again," "Never" is given emphasis by placing it at the beginning of the sentence.

epistolary plural is the use of the pronoun "we" ("us," "our") instead of "I" ("me," "my") in writing by a single person, for the purpose of achieving a more formal or impersonal effect. It is also called the "editorial 'we.'"

exclusive first person plural excludes the person(s) addressed. That is, a speaker may use "we" to refer to himself and his companions, while specifically excluding the person(s) to whom he is speaking. See inclusive.

explicit refers to information which is expressed in the words of a discourse. This is in contrast to implicit information. See implicit.

feminine is one of the Greek genders. See gender.

figure, figure of speech, or figurative expression involves the use of words in other than their literal or ordinary sense, in order to bring out some aspect of meaning by means of comparison or association. For example, "raindrops dancing on the street," or "his speech was like thunder." Metaphors and similes are figures of speech.

first person. See person.

future tense. See tense.

gender is any of the three grammatical subclasses of Greek nouns and pronouns (called masculine, feminine, and neuter), which determine agreement with and selection of other words or grammatical forms.

genitive case is a grammatical set of forms occuring in many languages, used primarily to indicate that a noun is the modifier of another noun. The genitive often indicates possession, but it may also indicate measure, origin, apposition, characteristic, separation, source, etc.

grammatical refers to grammar, which includes the selection and arrangement of words in phrases, clauses, and sentences.

imperative refers to forms of a verb which indicate commands or requests. In "Go and do likewise," the verbs "Go" and "do" are imperatives.

[ 169 ]

In most languages, imperatives are confined to the grammatical second person; but some languages have corresponding forms for the first and third persons. These are usually expressed in English by the use of "may" or "let"; for example, "May we not have to beg!" "Let them work harder!"

implicit (implied, implication) refers to information that is not formally represented in a discourse, since it is assumed that it is already known to the receptor, or evident from the meaning of the words in question. For example, the phrase "the other son" carries with it the implicit information that there is a son in addition to the one mentioned. This is in contrast to explicit information, which is expressly stated in a discourse. See explicit.

inclusive first person plural includes both the speaker and the one(s) to whom he is speaking. See exclusive.

indicative refers to forms of a verb in which an act or condition is stated or questioned as an actual fact rather than a potentiality or unrealized condition. The verb "won" in "The king won the battle" is in the indicative form.

ironical is having the quality of irony, which is a sarcastic or humorous manner of discourse in which what is said is intended to express its opposite; for example, "That was a wise thing to do!" when intended to convey the meaning, "That was a stupid thing to do!"

literal means the ordinary or primary meaning of a term or expression, in contrast with a figurative meaning. A literal translation is one which represents the exact words and word order of the source language; such a translation frequently is unnatural or awkward in the receptor language.

manuscripts are books, documents, letters, etc., written by hand. Thousands of manuscript copies of various Old and New Testament books still exist, but none of the original manuscripts. See copyists.

masculine is one of the Greek genders. See gender.

metaphor is likening one object, event, or state to another by speaking of it as if it were the other; for example, "flowers dancing in the breeze." Metaphors are the most commonly used figures of speech and are often so subtle that a speaker or writer is not conscious of the fact that he is using figurative language. See simile.

neuter is one of the Greek genders. See gender.

noun is a word that names a person, place, thing, idea, etc., and often serves to specify a subject or topic of a discourse.

object. See direct object.

parenthetical statement is a digression from the main theme of a discourse which interrupts that discourse. It is usually set off by marks of parenthesis ( ).

participle is a verbal adjective, that is, a word which retains some of the characteristics of a verb while functioning as an adjective. In "singing waters" and "painted desert," "singing" and "painted" are participles.

passive. See voice.

past tense. See tense.

perfect tense is a set of verb forms which indicate an action already completed when another action occurs. For example, in "John had finished his task when Bill came," "had finished" is in the perfect tense. The perfect tense in Greek also indicates that the action continues into the present. See also tense.

person, as a grammatical term, refers to the speaker, the person spoken to, or the person spoken about. First person is the person(s) speaking ("I," "me," "my," "mine," "we," "us," "our," "ours"). Second person is the person(s) or thing(s) spoken to ("thou," "thee," "thy," "thine," "ye," "you," "your," "yours"). Third person is the person(s) or thing(s) spoken about ("he," "she," "it," "his," "her," "them," "their," etc.). The examples here given are all pronouns, but in many languages the verb forms have affixes which indicate first, second, or third person and also indicate whether they are singular or plural.

phrase is a grammatical construction of two or more words, but less than a complete clause or a sentence. A phrase is usually given a name according to its function in a sentence, such as "noun phrase," "verb phrase," "prepositional phrase," etc.

plural refers to the form of a word which indicates more than one. See singular.

present tense. See tense.

pronouns are words which are used in place of nouns, such as "he," "him," "his," "she," "we," "them," "who," "which," "this," or "these."

receptor is the person(s) receiving a message. The receptor language is the language into which a translation is made. For example, in a translation from Hebrew into German, Hebrew is the source language and German is the receptor language.

restructure is to reconstruct or rearrange. See structure.

rhetorical question is an expression which is put in the form of a question but which is not intended to ask for information. Rhetorical questions are usually employed for the sake of emphasis.

sarcasm (sarcastic) is an ironical and frequently contemptous manner of discourse in which what is said is intended to express its opposite; for example, "That was a smart thing to do!" when intended to convey the meaning, "That was a stupid thing to do!"

second person. See person.

sentence is a grammatical construction composed of one or more clauses and capable of standing alone.

Septuagint is a translation of the Hebrew Old Testament into Greek, made some two hundred years before Christ. It is often abbreviated as LXX.

simile (pronounced SIM-i-lee) is a figure of speech which describes one event or object by compaing it to another, using "like," "as," or some other word to mark or signal the comparison. For example, "She runs like a deer," "He is as straight as an arrow." Similes are less subtle than metaphors in that metaphors do not mark the comparison with words such as "like" or "as." See metaphor.

singular refers to the form of a word which indicates one thing or person, in contrast to plural, which indicates more than one. See plural.

structure is the systematic arrangement of the elements of language, including the ways in which words combine into phrases, phrases into clauses, and clauses into sentences. Because this process may be compared to the building of a house or a bridge, such words as structure and construction are used in reference to it. To separate and rearrange the various components of a sentence or other unit of discourse in the translation process is to restructure it.

synonyms are words which are different in form but similar in meaning, such as "boy" and "lad." Expressions which have essentially the same meaning are said to be synonymous. No two words are completely synonymous.

tense is usually a form of a verb which indicates time relative to a discourse or some event in a discourse. The most common forms of tense are past, present, and future. See also perfect tense.

transitional expressions are words or phrases which mark the connections between related events. Some typical transitionals are "next," "then," "later," "after this," "when he arrived."

translation is the reproduction in a receptor language of the closest natural equivalent of a message in the source language, first, in terms of meaning, and second, in terms of style.

verbs are a grammatical class of words which express existence, action, or occurrence, such as "be," "become," "run," or "think."

versions are translations. The ancient, or early, versions are translations of the Bible, or of portions of the Bible, made in early times;
for example, the Greek Septuagint, the ancient Syriac, or the Ethiopic
versions.

voice in grammar is the relation of the action expressed by a verb to
the participants in the action. In English and many other languages,
the active voice indicates that the subject performs the action ("John
hit the man"), while the passive voice indicates that the subject is
being acted upon ("The man was hit").

# Index

This index includes concepts, key words, and terms for which the Guide contains a discussion useful for translators.

Printed in the United States of America